The Message
of the Stars.

Introductory

Having learned to cast a horoscope the next, and most important part is to read its message. Astrology means "star Logic" and we most seriously advise the student not to depend too much on authorities but to try to understand the basic nature of each planet, the influence of signs, houses and aspects; then by a process of reasoning to combine these and thus develope his own intuition which will serve him far better than the ability to quote like a Poll Parrot what some one else has said.

We would also advise the young Astrologer not to bother too much with the personal descriptions indicated in the horoscope, it is foolish to spend hours perhaps to find out, what the one for whom a horoscope is cast can see in a moment by looking in a glass. We give descriptions of the different types, but do so for the purpose of aiding the student to determine at sight the probable sign and planet rising when a client comes who does not know his birth hour. There are people for instance, who have the face of a sheep just as perfect as possible. If such a one is in doubt about the birth hour we would at once look to Aries and experimentally try how that would fit with the other characteristics of that person, if we did so, we should probably find our guess correct in every case.

Thus also the other signs and planets in signs exhibit distinguishing characteristics of valuable aid to the student in the direction mentioned.

The student should also endeavor to cultivate perfect confidence in the science of Astrology. There is **nothing empirical about character reading and diagnosis,** in those respects it is plain as ABC. **Predictions may fail** because the Astrologer is unable to determine the strength of will of the person for whom he predicts, but the latent tendencies are always accurately foreshown. The writers have found that where they do not personally know the people whose characters they read, their delineations are much deeper and more accurate because then personal bias and impressions are absent and the mystic scroll of the heavens more easily read.

Aries, the Ram

Aries is mythologically represented as a Ram and the symbol describes most accurately those born under its influence, a pointed and protruding sheeplike nose, wide forehead, pointed chin, and the resultant triangular face noted in many people, are unmistakable indications of their rising sign, light brown or reddish tint of the hair is a pronounced characteristic of the Aries, the body is slender and well formed, if the first of the sign is rising the body is shorter, and the complexion darker than given by the latter degrees.

Planets in the rising sign will modify the description, however, and the student must use his knowledge of the character of the planets in conjunction with the description of the Sign. The Sun and Mars make the complexion more florid, the Moon and Saturn make it paler and darker, Jupiter and Venus make the body more portly. Saturn shortens, Uranus and Mercury lengthen it. This applies to all the signs, but is specially marked when a planet rises in the sign it rules. Mars, in Aries **rising** would give fiery red hair and a face full of freckles, the Sun rising in Leo would give a florid complexion with flaxen hair, but if Saturn were there, instead it would shorten the body and darken the hair.

Aries people are bold, selfconfident and impulsive; they aim to lead, dislike to follow, are always ready to take the initiative in any movement that appeals to them, but often lack persistence to carry their projects to a conclusion over serious obstacles.

The Sun, and Mars the ruler, rising in Aries would intensify the above, but as a thorough explanation has been given under the heading: "The intrinsic natures of the Planets," the student is referred thereto, we may mention here however, as a peculiarity that Aries people live through fevers when others succumb. We have known their hair to fall out, and the temperature to remain four degrees above maximum for many hours, without fatal result.

Taurus, the Bull

Taurus is represented by a Bull in the Zodiac, and the bodies generated under this sign are usually short and stocky. They have a strong neck with the bump of Amativeness well developed, large lobe of the ear, heavy jaws, full face; nose short and stubby. Dark eyes and wavy hair frequently give them considerable beauty. The eye of the Taurian may never dart bolts of fire such as those wherewith the Arian would anihilate his enemies, it is softer, but under provocation it becomes sullenly expressive of the passive resistance wherewith these people win their battles. It then marks the difference between the impulsive Aries and the stubborn Taurus. The inner phalange of the thumb is large and heavy, the calves well developed and the foot chubby. In walking the Taurian usually plants his heel first, and heaviest.

Taurus people are pre-eminently "thorough and steadfast" in everything they do: In love, in hate, in work or play, they persist in a given direction, and neither reason nor argument will turn them. They are verbose and argumentative in defense of their actions or opinions; they grasp new ideas slowly, with difficulty and conservatively, but once comprehended, and espoused, they always remember what they have learned and defend their opinion to the last ditch.

The Sun rising in Taurus gives an unusually fine physique, and accentuates the Taurus pride in strength. **The Moon,** being the planet of fecundity, is exalted in this exceedingly fruitful sign; hence people with the Moon in Taurus, have large families, particularly if the configuration is in the 5th House, for that designates children.

Venus, the ruler of Taurus rising in that sign, makes the form beautiful as well as strong, it also gives artistic ability and musical inspiration.

Gemini, the Twins

When Gemini is rising the body generated is tall and slender; the arms and limbs are particularly long, fingers slender, hair dark, eyes hazel. Gemini people are quick, active and alert in all their movements, habitual resltessness is noticeable in the expression of the eye which differs in that respect from more fixed tendencies of the eyes of those born under the two preceeding signs, although of course we do not mean that the Arian always looks angry and the Taurian stubborn, nevertheless, there is a settled tendency in those directions noticeable when these people are not occupied in a certain direction, but the Gemini person has an expression which is much more vivid, changeable and past finding out. They have acutely enquiring minds, always want to know the reason why, but often lack persistence to follow clews to the end, and thus meet disappointment. Being tactful they avoid giving offense even under provocation, and are therefore generally liked by all; though their

own affections are not deep. Two distinct classes
are born under this sign, one, too fond of reading,
should cultivate independent thought, instead of re-
peating other peoples ideas, or aping their manners;
the other is scientific, well balanced and reserved;
a model for any person.

The Sun rising in Gemini brings out all the nobl-
est traits of the sign, it makes the nature more settled and contented, gives more persistence and a
particularly healthy and active body.

Mercury, the ruler, rising in Gemini sharpens
perception, gives ability as a writer, or speaker,
but makes the person born with that configuration
extremely irritable vaccillating, fond of change of
scene and employment. They are best fitted for
traveling salesmen.

Cancer, the Crab

The chief peculiarities of the crab are a clumsy
body, slender limbs and powerful claws; people
born with Cancer rising express them all. They
have a large upper body, augmented in later years
by a prominence of the abdomen acquired by over-
eating. The mandible or lower Jaw is powerfully
hinged to the cranium, the face is therefore widest
between the ears, the mouth is also large, and the
whole construction similar to the crabs claw. The
face is full, the hair brown, the eyes blue, complexion pale and sickly, for the Cancer person has
the least vitality of any. The limbs are extremely
slender in proportion to the large upper body, so
the structure appears 'top heavy,' and they walk
with a "rolling" gait.

Cancer people are very fond of the home and
its comforts, they are quiet, reserved and adapt
themselves to conditions, hence they are easy to
get along with, their anger is shortlived, and they
hold no spite. Though lacking in physical prowess,
they are no hypocrites, but always have the courage of their convictions, they voice and defend them

too. For that reason, though they sometimes win a place in public life, they are not successful, particularly as they are sensitive of personal criticisms.

The Sun rising in Cancer brings out and accentuates all the good qualities mentioned above, it gives more ambition and pride; also increases the vitality, and is a particular boon to people with Cancer rising in that respect, on account of their very low life force. Cancer, with its ruler the Moon, governs the stomach and hence alimentation, Leo and its ruler, the Sun, have charge of the heart and circulation. If these signs and planets are well placed in the horoscope, they conteract most other afflictions and a long lease of life is assured, but if they are afflicted, much sickness results unless intelligent care is applied to modify the omen.

The Moon, the ruler, rising in Cancer will give much instability to the nature, and Jupiter being exalted will bring fortune and fame.

Leo, the Lion

The Lion is the king of beasts and even in captivity is an embodiment of stateliness and pride. The typical Leo's of the Zodiac also express pride in every movement and stateliness, which will not escape attention of the keen observer, the expansive chest, the massive shoulders, the strong arm and the large head contrast considerably with the more slender but still muscular under body, and as Aries has the sheep face, so the typical Leo has certain feline features. The complexion is florid, eyes large and full, blue or grayish in color, they express laughter, cheerfulness and content. The whole frame is well knit and strong, having great endurance and recuperative power.

Leo rules the heart, and it is a marked characteristic that people with Leo rising unafflicted, have hearts bigger than their pocketbooks, they give generously of their time, money, or knowledge without thought of self. If the Sun rises in Leo, this trait becomes almost prodigality, but if Saturn is there to afflict instead, he will counteract it so that they will either circumscribe their gifts with conditions to such an extent that they retain practical control, or they will spend their means on themselves.

Leos are honest and faithful; being children of the Daystar, they love light and truth, are above subterfuge and aim straight at their object. Their will is firm to attain by honorable means. They make good orators and hold their audiences by personal magnetism. They are very attractive to the opposite sex, and the lower nature should be held firmly in check, otherwise serious trouble and heartache may ensue. The French, as a race, are ruled by Leo, and afford ample illustration of this point.

The Sun rising in Leo, unafflicted, gives a body of wonderful strength, vitality and recuperative power; superior in its wiriness to the body generated by the Sun in Taurus; but if Mars afflicts, palpitation of the heart will ensue. Saturn will cause regurgitation unless care is taken in early years to avoid strain.

Virgo, the Virgin

People born when Virgo is rising, are above middle stature, slender in youth, but with a pronounced tendency to prominence of abdomen in later years. The upper part of the head is much more developed than the lower, the weak chin, showing lack of will and the large brain indicating greatness of intellect are therefore earmarks of the Virgo. The face is thin, the complexion sallow, the hair brown and the eyes hazel or grey. The feet are small, the toes turn inwards and give these people a peculiar labored walk.

Virgo people are very quick and active in youth, they learn with facility, but do not work hard for knowledge; they seem to breathe it in without an effort. They acquire linguistic and elocutionary powers most readily, are fluent writers but often cynical, cold and unforgiving when they have been injured. In later years "Health" becomes a disease with them, they are extreme in their food, and make hygiene a fad; they fancy that they have every imaginable disease, because Virgo is the sixth sign and has a certain affinity with the sixth House, denoting Health and Disease.

It is peculiar, that while the Sun lends vitality, and brings out the best in all the other signs, he accentuates* this deplorable characteristic in the Virgo.

Mercury, the ruler ,is also exalted here, and gives pronouncement of all the good which otherwise might be expected from the Sun.

Libra, the Scales

Elegance, may be said to express in one word, the physical peculiarities of the Libran. The body is slender and graceful in youth; it becomes more plump as life advances, but even the portliness of the Libra body is pleasing. The complexion is smooth and clear, eyes are soft and blue with a kind expression; the mouth is unusually well formed and the teeth particularly fine and even.

Libra people have extremely strong conjugal affection, so strong, in fact, that it overshadows all other considerations. The Leos love their families; but their hearts take in all the world besides, not so the Librans, they are ready for any sacrifice to give comforts to those in their own immediate home circle but they are also prepared to sacrifice anyone elses family for their own, if necessary.

In most other traits the Librans express aptly the symbolism of their sign: a pair of scales, and their characteristics might be expressed in the word: "Changeability." They are people of "moods," because Saturn is exalted here and weighs upon the mind; the changes are sudden and extreme; they may follow a fad with as much zest as if their life depended upon it, and then, without a moments warning, drop it and take up something entirely opposite; there are no halfway measures in the swing of the scales. Being naturally given to change, they are most adaptable to circumstances, and do not fret over reverses, but set about to restore their fortunes with vim and vigor.

Aries and Libra may be said to be the battle-fields of the Sun and Saturn: Life and Death, Joy and Sorrow. The Sun is exalted in Aries, and vanquishes Saturn; hence the intrepidity of Aries people. In Libra the scales tip the other way, there Saturn is exalted, and conquers the Sun; this gives a softer tone to the Libran; whose kindly politeness contrasts markedly with the Arians brusque address. Venus, the ruler of Libra is not alone responsible for this trait, for Taurus people are blunt, though Venus rules. Venus rising in Libra gives artistic ability, Saturn turns the mind in scientific directions.

Scorpio, the Eagle

The nose is the most prominent feature of the Scorpio; it is large, heavy, and hooked, resembling the bill of the eagle; the brows are bushy, the eyes sharp and piercing; the jaw is very heavy; the glint of the eye, and the set of the jaw indicate the great determination which is the most prominent characteristic of the Scorpio. The face is angular, complexion murky, and hair dark, with a peculiar ruddy tinge noticeable when the sun shines on it. The teeth are large and subject to early decay. The body is short and thickset, with a short, thick neck resembling that of the opposite sign: Taurus.

Scorpio people always stand up for their rights, and never submit to imposition, though prone to ride roughshod over others. They are full of worries over things that may happen, but never do, and thus make life a burden to those around them.

Sarcasm that stings like a scorpion is aye upon the tip of their tongue, yet their love is strong, and their aspirations lofty. Thus there are two natures struggling in the Scorpio and they need much sympathy and forbearance from their friends. In the hour of danger they never flinch; but perform deeds of heroism with a disregard of self that amounts to foolhardiness; the mind is sharp, cool and collected, therefore Scorpio men make good army officers and *excel* in surgery. The Scorpio woman has a large family.

The Sun in Scorpio accentuates the good traits, and gives a love of Mysticism; but Mars, the ruler. brings out the worldly side of the sign, it makes scoffers and sceptics.

Saggitarius, the Centaur

People born with Saggitarius rising are even taller than those born under the opposite sign: Gemini, the men in particular have large hands and feet. The size and weight of the bony frame is often too much for the ligaments of the spine to support, and so these people develop a decided stoop in later years. The face is long and well formed, the nose well proportioned, dark kindly eyes, with dark chestnut hair. The body is very active, but requires much rest, as the recuperative powers are below the requisite.

The symbol of this sign shows that there are two widely different classes born therein. One, designated by the animal body of the Centaur, is frankly in for "a good time," they are sporty, soldiers of fortune, of roving proclivities, fond of games of chance, and ready to risk their all on the turn of a card, the speed of a horse, or a game of ball, but while Aries or Scorpio people may become pugilists, and Taurus people take up wrestling as a profession, the sports of Saggitarius have no element of cruelty in them, sometimes when afflicted they may be criminals, their crimes are never violent, however, but rather results of their indulgence of the animal nature.

The other Class is the extreme opposite; symbolized by the human part of the sign. Here is the man rising above the animal nature, bending the bow of aspiration and aiming at limitless space; signifying the loftiest longings of that immortal spark of incipient divinity we call the soul. Law abiding, of the highest morals, honored pillars in the church; beloved rulers of state, famed for integrity, benevolence and justice.

The Sun rising in this sign is sure to bring preferment even to those born in lowly and obscure circumstances, and accentuate all good shown in the sign; so will Jupiter, the ruler.

Capricorn, the Goat

Capricorn rising gives a short, slender, narrow-chested body with a thin neck, thin silky dark hair, a pale peaked face with small blinking weak eyes. The chin pointed and turned upwards, the nose pointed and turned downwards, an impediment in the speech, illformed lower limbs and an awkward walk. The vitality is very low, and these children are reared with great difficulty, but once infancy is past, they exhibit a tenacity that is truly amazing, and often become very, very old; they seem to dry up into a mass of wrinkled skin and bone that is all but imperishable, this, on account of the Saturn ray which rules Capricorn. It is noticeable also, that all who have that planet prominent in the nativity show the before mentioned wrinkling of the skin; even though they may retain corpulence conferred by other configurations.

Ambition and Suspicion are ruling characteristics, an inordinate desire for recognition of their claims to superiority and advancement, also suspicion that others are trying to subvert or withhold the coveted prize, are ever with these people. It causes them much unnecessary worry; and may result in habitual melancholy, particularly if Saturn is afflicted. They ought to seek amusement outdoors, read funny stories and otherwise try to cultivate a sense of the humorous from childhood, for this is one of the saddest signs, and needs all possible encouragement.

Capricorn people are successful in detective work, where secret, practices are used to trap others; and persistence is required to ferret out a mystery, for they never give up. The afflicted Capricorn is very revengeful, and if by Mars, may shed blood to satisfy a grudge. The Sun rising brings out the Justice, Purity and honor of the sign makes Captains of Construction such as forward the great enterprises of the world.

Aquarius, the Water Bearer

The stateliness and pride of those born under the sign Leo are not missing in the typical Aquarian, but while in the Leo these qualities are of a lower, more beastly nature agreeable to the sign, they are manly pride and manly stateliness in the true Aquarian. Libra generates a beautiful body but more effeminate as it were, whereas the Aquarian beauty is truly manly or womanly, the fearless eye is kindly and drooping eyelashes are peculiar to this sign. The forehead is square, and the well developed poise tells of intellect, the large domed head shows the spiritual side of the nature and the chin is sufficiently developed to give purpose to all actions. Thus the typical Aquarian is the highest grade of humanity; but therefore, also exceedingly rare, for the variants produced in each sign from the typical, by the interposition of one or more planets are so different that the type is often unrecognizable in the majority of its features. Aquarians are most loyal to friends, therefore they attract many, keep them through life, and are much benefitted by them. Like Capricorn, this sign is ruled by Saturn, and he gives to the Aquarian the same retiring nature and tendency to melancholy which marks the Capricornian, but also the persistence in following a given course, and whatever financial success comes to these people is the result of continued and patient effort; Aquarians are very deliberate and longsuffering; they never act in a hurry, and therefore seldom have cause to regret their actions, save when reason has been stilled through play upon their sympathies, for under such circumstances they are readily imposed upon. The love of nature is very strong but they are not as demonstrative as the Leo. It is noteworthy that the qualities of opposite signs are always reflected: Leo in Aquarians, reflects love; Taurus mirrors the passion of Scorpio, the Gemini body is a reflex of the bony Saggitarius frame, etc.

Both the Sun and Saturn bring out more prominently the good traits of Aquarius, for this sign where Saturn rules, and Libra, where it is exalted, are therefore under its most benign influence. The Sun in Aquarius adds much hope and life to the nature, and thus counteracts the melancholy trait previously mentioned.

Pisces, the Fishes

The typical Piscean is short, flabby and fleshy with a waddling gait not unlike those born under the sign Cancer, but differs from them by having a stouter body. The feet are very often turned in but larger than those born under Virgo. The body is weak and deficient in recuperative force. The complexion is medium, the eyes blue, watery and expressionless, the nose is large and flat.

There is a strong tendency to mediumship among the Pisces people, and therein is a danger greater than any other on earth, no one should "sit for development" and degenerate into the tool of low spirits, but a Pisces person in particular is "lost" if taken control of. They cannot free themselves, neither in this life or the next, because generically inert and devoid of will power. They are timid, and even the men are tearful on the slightest provocation, they love leisure more than comfort, and do not work when not absolutely necessary to keep body and soul together, they love change of scene, rove about considerably, generally in an aimless manner. Being fond of good things to eat and drink, particularly the latter, and lacking will to curb their appetite when afflicted, they frequently indulge their craving to such an extent that they become habitual drunkards.

The Sun rising in Pisces gives more energy and ambition, Jupiter, the ruler, strengthens the morals, and Venus exalted in this sign, gives great musical talent, but accentuates the tendency to alcoholic indulgence, which mars the lives of so many splendid musicians.

The Intrinsic Nature of the Planets

The nature of gun powder which causes it to explode under certain circumstances is neither good nor bad, the quality of its action is determined by the way its power is used, when it furthers the welfare of the community it is called good, and evil when used in a manner derogatory to our well being, so also with the planets, they are neither good nor evil, each has its intrinsic nature and acts in a manner consonant therewith save as modified by the circumstances under which its powers are exerted. When we know the nature of a sign and the nature of a planet, we may combine the two, and thus obtain the correct reading of the stellar script by our own reasoning instead of depending upon authorities, for instance, the Sun is hot, full of vital force, and exercises an influence that buoys us up in a body and spirit, when its rays fall upon us with moderate strength, it makes us stronger and more cheerful, for there is an atmosphere of generosity, out-going love and kindliness in the Sun. Thus if the Sun at birth is in the weak sign

Cancer, naturally the effect would be to modify the
constitution described in the foregoing list of the
signatures of the signs; the heat of the Sun would
give a more florid complexion to the Cancer person,
the general health and recuperative powers would
be materially augmented not to speak of the changes
that would be manifested in the disposition, giving
more ambition, hopefulness and buoyancy to the
temperament. Suppose on the other hand, that
the Sun is in Aries when that sign is rising at the
birth of a person, then the fire of the Sun, added to
the fire of the sign Aries, will increase the boldness
and the intrepidity of the person to such a degree
that it may become foolhardiness, particularly, if
Mars, the ruler of Aries, is also there and increases
the warlike tendencies, those are characteristics, but
the physical body will also suffer from this excessive heat, the blood will race through the veins of
such a person like a Niagara of liquid fire, and
fevers would be a frequent experience, as the super-
abundance of vitality burns out the physical case-
ment. Were the cold, slow and sluggish Saturn
there instead of the Sun and Mars, he might
squelch almost all of the Aries characteristics both
mental and physical. If we consider Aries symbolized by a stove in which a fire is burning, it
would make the same difference whether the hot
Mars, or the cold Saturn, were placed there, as it
makes a difference whether we pour oil or water
into the stove. Similarly all the other planets produce various results, according to their intrinsic
natures; and their various combinations. For the
sake of lucidity, and ready reference, let us first
set down the word which describes best the most
salient characteristics of each planet.

The Sun	Life	Neptune	Divinity
The Moon	Fecundation	Saturn	Obstruction
Venus	Coalition	Mars	Dynamic Energy
Mercury	Reason	Uranus	Altruism
	Jupiter	Idealism	

After the student has learned the reasons why we ascribe the characteristic embodied in the keyword to each planet, he may easily reason out its effect in any and all cases, and be his own authority instead of quoting us or anyone else.

The Sun
(Life)

The Sun, being the center of the solar system is recognized by all as the physical lifegiver, even when they do not believe in anything superphysical; it is patent to everyone from personal observation, that the horizontal ray of the morning sun, affects us differently from the perpendicular noonray, and that in summer the rays carry a life force which not only brings forth the verdure upon the fields, but also affects the human temperament, and endows us with vital energy, courage and a hopeful spirit foreign to the dark and gloomy winter months. This gloom is permanently noticeable in the temperament of people living in the far north, where the absence of sunlight makes life a struggle, that saps the spirit of frolic, while in countries where abundance of sunlight lessens the care of existence the temperament is correspondingly vivacious, hopeful and sunny.

In the horoscope, the angle of each planetary ray at birth, determines the department in life it will affect. If the child is born at the noon hour, when the sun is at Zenith, the daystar will appear in the 10th house of the horoscope, and bring preferment professionally. If the child were born at midnight, when the sun is directly under the place of birth, its influence would be through the 4th House, and it would brighten the old age of the child then born.

There are three unfortunate angles for the sun: Children born shortly after sunset have it in the sixth House, which indicates sickness, and as the sun is lifegiver, this position lessens the vitality and recuperative power. Birth in the middle part of the afternoon places the sun in the 8th House.

This is the house through which the deathdealing forces act, and logically, the Lord of Life is out of place in the House of death. The 2nd House shows what income we obtain by our own efforts, and as the 8th House is opposite the 2nd, it reveals the sources of revenue for which we do not personally exert, ourselves, that is to say: legacies, stipends, pensions or grants of a public nature. We have known people with the sun in the 8th House to acquire vast sums, millions in one case, by speculation in municipal necessities. Such persons are often threatened by death, and sometimes have many hairbreadth escapes, but even with the best of aspects to the Sun, a ripe age is seldom attained.

When a child is born shortly after sunrise, the Sun is in the 12th House, which is the avenue whence we reap our sorrows, and it has been our experience that the early life of such a person is encompassed by trouble, of one kind or another, until progression of the Ascendant brings the Sun into the first House,—roughly speaking, one year for every degree the Sun is above the Ascendant. Poverty, sickness and trouble in the parental home attend this configuration, and we have found this measure of great value in determining the true Ascendant where the time was not accurately known.

Saturn

(Obstruction)

A fruitful method of acquiring knowledge is by comparison of similars and contrast of opposites; thus lights and sidelights are brought out, which otherwise may escape attention.

Applying this method to the Sun and Saturn, we remember that the key word of the Sun is "Life," and at the vernal equinox when the Sun is in Aries, the sign of its exaltation, we may readily note the powerful effect of the crestwave of vital fluid then poured over the earth, Nature is vibrant with life, which races through the forms of all kingdoms and endues them with such abundance of vitality, that they are compelled to generate in order to take care of the overflow; Life manifests as motion; but the keynote of Saturn is Obstruction, therefore that is the planet of decrepitude and decay, and consequently, when the Sun is in Libra, the sign of Saturn's exaltation, at the fall equinox, Nature is tired and ready for its wintry sleep. The human frame also is energized by the solar life contained in our food, which enters our system through the region governed by the Suns exaltation sign:—the head, and is eliminated by the activity of the liver and kidneys ruled by Saturn and his exaltation sign.

In youth, when the Sun forces surge through the frame a superabundant force sweeps obstructions aside, assimilation and excretion balance, but as Time goes on, "Chronos" or Saturn accumulates obstructions in the organs of excretion, and elimination is gradually restricted, the avenues of life are dammed up, and decrepitude and decay turn the scales of life, (Libra), towards the realm of death.

Similarly in other departments of life; where the Sun makes the social favorite, by imbuing us with optimism and a bright sunny smile, Saturn makes recluses and sours existence with frowns and pessimism; where the Sun furthers our worldly affairs and makes things run smooth, Saturn causes provoking delays of the most inexplicable nature; all the world seems to conspire to frustrate our plans.

The lash of Saturn is not pleasant, we sometimes chafe, fret and fume while being thus held in leash, but meanwhile we ripen and are more fitted, when the obstruction is removed, to have or use that which Saturn delayed, for as we develop physical muscle by overcoming physical obstacles, so we cultivate soul power by the resistance spiritually engendered by Saturn, the teaching which he gives

may be summed up in the motto: "Patient persistence in well doing."

Venus
(Coalition)

Coalition is the act or process of drawing together separate particles or units, and causing them
to sink differences and to amalgamate into a united
whole.   Goethe, the inspired seer who wrote the
novel, "Elective Affinities," there compares the loves
and hates of atoms to the loves and hates of human
beings, and he is right, it is the Venus ray which
unites microbe and man alike; it inspires the beast
and bird with love for their young, only in smaller
measure than the mother love which nurtured us
through helpless infancy. In whatever house Venus
is located she will exercise an influence tending to
smooth out difficulties and maintain Harmony and
Rhythm.   Thus in the first House she will aim to
spread sunshine over the childhoods home, sweeten
the disposition and make the early life happy.   In
the third House which signifies brothers and sis-
ters, Venus harmonizes them and you may conclude
that you have earned this love by kindness in a
previous Existence. The seventh House being concerned with marriage, she will fill our life with conjugal love of the tenderest nature, if this is the angle
of her expression. From the 11th House Venus
will attract kind friends whose affections we have
won before, for the horoscope shows what we have
earned, joy or sorrow, WE have made our "luck,"
the stars only mark the time to reap, as the Sun
calls the harvestman, and the kindness of friends today was enlisted yester-life by our helpful acts.
Nor can we keep friends, life partners or relatives
in bonds of affection unless we constantly feed the
fires of love, for no matter how well Venus is placed,
the planets show only the trend of things, this
tendency WE have made and WE can also mar it,
similarly in the other Houses except the House of

sorrow, there the smile of love is drowned in tears. When Venus ray is afflicted, it curtails the sense of beauty and order; hence the person becomes slothful, disorderly and lacking in proper self-respect. Incapable, because of the affliction, of feeling the true love, such persons become perverted and licentious; and it is often said of such, "He is his own worst enemy."

Mars

(Dynamic Energy)

Power may be latent for milleniums as exemplified in the coalbeds which are reservoirs of solar force; a furnace and engine are required to transmute and make it available as dynamic energy, but, once the sleeping giant has been roused from latency to potency it knows no rest or peace till it has expended the last ounce of its prodigious strength. Under strict control, and carefully guided into channels of useful activity, this fiery force is the most valuable servant of mankind; the most powerful agent in the world's work, an incomparable boon to humanity. But if it escapes control the servant quickly takes mastery, its inimical power of destruction and devastation is then as terrible a scourge, as its beneficent use under guidance is an inestimable blessing. It is as precious as it is dangerous, eternal vigilance is the price of safety from its ravages, but without it the world would be a wilderness.

Mars, as a focus for the latent solar life, transmutes it into desire, passion and what we may call animal spirits. It is a consuming fire, more dangerous than all the nitroglycerine ever manufactured, but also more precious than any other blessing we can have or enjoy.

The Hindoo preacher, nurtured in a land governed by Saturn, the planet of obstruction, says: "Kill out desire," he dreams away his days in destitution, but as "temper" conserves the edge of the steel that carves its way through all obstructions, so the well-directed energetic desires of the martial Anglo Saxon has wrought a marvelous transformation in the earth, it has reared a civilization beyond all which preceded it, and though perhaps brutal in many respects, there is promise in that also, according to the proverb: "The greater the sinner, the greater the saint." Parents should take a lesson from the book of nations and refrain from applying the Saturnine wet blanket to the fiery Mars spirit of children. Saturn always says don't, don't, his aim is to repress and obstruct. A clear fire under proper control is useful, but death lurks in the smoke and noxious gases of a smothered fire; too many don'ts smother legitimate ambition and frustrate ambition and frustrate accomplishment, they may drive the hapless victim into ways of evil for the dynamic energy of Mars must and will have an outlet, so beware. The worst faults of Mars are impulsiveness and lack of persistence, but he breeds no hypocrites like an afflicted Saturn.

Mercury

(Reason)

As Mars brings the solar life to a focus in desire and emotion, so Mercury is the focus through which the faculty of reason in the human being, finds expression to act as a curb upon the lower nature and assist in lifting us from the human to the divine. Being the messenger of the Gods, the other planets, it has no voice of its own, and is more dependent for expression upon the aspects of other planets than even the moon, many may and do feel deeply, they may also have valuable knowledge, but they are unable to give it expression or share it with others, for lack of aspects to Mercury. Even a so-called evil aspect helps to bring out what is within, and what is the result of aspects between Mercury and the other planets is easily seen by coupling the keywords with a mental attitude.

Good aspects to Mars would bring dynamic energy to the mind, make it extremely active, quick and keen, ready to take the initiative in new projects. Evil aspects make an erratic person, a demagogue, an agitator, and is liable to bring conflict with the law, specially if in Taurus or Scorpio, the sting of their tongue is as the poison of a serpent.

Mars may give initiative, and start us precipitately upon a certain course of action which later developments force us to abandon, but where good aspects of Saturn and Mercury prevail, forethought measures obstructions carefully before launching upon any venture, the start may be slow, but once a course of action has been decided upon, it is certain that the persistence of Saturn will surmount all obstacles and carry the matter to a satisfactory conclusion. These aspects denote the deep thinker, the honest judge, or diplomat, the capable adviser. Evil aspects of Saturn and Mercury bring the keynote "obstruction" to the front, as ultra conservatism, narrowmindedness or a tendency to scheme how to take undue advantage of others, but while the impulsive Mars-Mercury criminal is usually caught in the net of the law, the shrewdness and underhanded cunning of the Saturn-Mercury offender almost invariably saves him, he may even be a respected member of the community he fleeces.

Fecundation is the keyword of the Moon, and Life is the intrinsic nature of the Sun. Aspects from the luminaries to Mercury therefore fertilize and enliven the mentality, even the so-called evil aspects are better than none.

The keynote of Venus is Coalition, hence its good aspects to Mercury make the clubman, the "good fellow" of Bohemian tastes, the artist, musician and social entertainer.

Good aspects of Jupiter and Mercury give a kindly, benevolent turn to the mind. Humane judges, orators of idealistic nature, business men of integrity and all who aim at social and civic ideals.

Jupiter
(Idealism)

It is said that "Opportunity knocks at every man's door," yet we often hear people bewail their fate because they "never had a chance." "Saturn" is blamed for our misfortunes when we have learned to study Astrology, we are so intently on the look out for evil that we usually forget to look for the good, and thus miss our opportunity. It takes Saturn 30 years to go around the horoscope, by transit, and form aspects to all planets, but Jupiter, the most beneficent influence in the solar system, goes around once in eleven years and thus the good fortunes which he may bring are at least three times as numerous as the misfortunes brought by Saturn's evil aspects.

As a matter af fact, we get from others just what we give, each is surrounded by a subtle auric atmosphere which colors our views of others, and the thoughts, ideas and actions of others towards us. If we harbor meanness in our hearts, that colors this atmosphere so that we see meanness in others and in their actions towards us, we awaken this trait in them, as vibrations from a tuningfork starts another of the same pitch to sing. On the other hand, if we cultivate the Jupiterian qualities of benevolence, his expansive smile, his cordial attitude of mind, etc., we shall soon feel the response in our circle of acquaintances and the beneficent aspect of Jupiter will then have greater effect in making our life and work pleasant.

Uranus
(Altruism)

Love is a much hackneyed word, but when we analyse it, that which is so-called is often so tainted with passion that it is really a Martial emotion and not Venusian. Mother love, which has been extolled as the purest aspect of this feelinig, is also to a great extent selfish, for it loves the child to evoke a return of the affection, but Altruism is a love that embraces all that breathes; an emotion such as that felt by the Christ when He wept over Jerusalem and bemoaned the fact that they would not accept His all enfolding Love. Seeing that that is so, we may readily understand that the great majority of our humanity cannot yet respond to the higher side of Uranus and its effects upon the morals are therefore principally perversion of sex, clandestine love affairs, free love, and disregard of convenionalities.

When Uranus is well aspected and strong, it gives high ideals, far beyond the understanding of the masses; this makes pioneers along progressive lines of thought, such as the Rosicrucian and kindred movements. On the Asc: he produces what are vulgarly termed "freaks" who aim at reform in dress, food, etc., totally disregarding commonly accepted ideas.

Uranus rules the ether, and when with Mercury or the Moon it brings the person in intimate touch with the electrical forces; it gives intuitive understanding and abhorrence of reason. The effects of Uranus are extremely sudden, and as we respond most readily to its evil side, these effects are generally felt to be disastrous.

Neptune

(Divinity

As Uranus is the octave of Venus and acts principally upon the love nature, aiming to elevate mankind in matters personal and social, so Neptune is the octave of Mercury, and altogether spiritual in its aims. As Mercury is Lightbearer of the physical Sun, so Neptune is Lightbearer for the spiritual Sun, (called Vulcan by the Western Mystics). Intellectuality, ruled by Mercury lifted us above the animal and made man man, the Spirituality ruled by Neptune will in time raise us beyond the estate of the human and make us divine.

Neptune really signifies what we may call "the gods," commencing with the supernormal beings we know as Elder Brothers, and compassing the innumerable hosts of spiritual entities, good, bad, and indifferent, which influence our evolution. Its position and aspects denote our relation to them, if any; malefic aspects attract agencies of a nature inimical to our welfare, benefic configurations draw upon the good forces. Thus, if Neptune is placed in the 10th House, trine to the ascendant, the person involved will have the opportunity to become a leader or prominent in a movement along mystical lines as denoted by the exalted position of Neptnue. His body will be capable of receiving the finer vibrations, and coming in touch with the spiritual world, as denoted by the trine of the ascendant. On the other hand, when Neptune is placed in the 12th House, whose nature is passive and productive of suffering, that position indicates that at some time, perhaps under a square from the midheaven, the evil forces, among whom are spirit-controls, will be drawn to that person and endeavor to obtain possession of the body. The conjunction of Neptnue with the ascendant will make the body sensitive and useable for spiritual purposes, as well as the trine. Given the opportunity afforded by the first aspect mentioned, the man may become a pupil of a mystery school and a factor for great good in the uplift of mankind; placed under the affliction of the second aspect, he may become a helpless tool of spirit-controls: an irresponsible medium.

But there is one factor which is never shown in the horoscope, and that is the will of the man. He is bound at some time in life to meet with the experiences denoted by his horoscope, and the opportunity there indicated will be placed before him one by one in orderly succession, as the clock of destiny marks the appropriate time; but how he, the free and independent spirit, meets that fated experience, no one can determine beforehand, and the man in whose horoscope the first mentioned benefic configuration occurs may not be sufficiently awake to the great opportunity before him to catch it on the wing, it may have flown before he realizes that it was there. Yes, he may never become aware of the fact. On the other hand, the person in whose life the square indicates the assault by spiritual forces mentioned, may develop his spiritual muscle by resisting the onslaught and become a victor instead of being vanquished. Forwarned is forarmed.

In the foregoing, the essential nature of the planets have been given, where they are well aspected by another planet these natural characteristics are enhanced so far as the benefic planets are concerned, but when evilly aspected, the nature of Venus, which is love and rhythm, becomes folly, licentiousness and sloth; the philosophy, law-abiding tendencies, mercy and lofty aspirations of Jupiter turn into lawlessness, disregard of others, and low pursuits; the lofty spirituality of the Sun will express itself as just animal spirits and physical health. In regard to the planets of the lower nature, good aspects of Mars turn the desires toward constructive objects, and well regulated activities, while evil aspects are responsible for the destructive expression of the desire nature. Saturn, when well aspected, gives mechanical and executive ability capable of directing the desire nature. It shows the brainy, persevering man able to cope with, and conquer, material obstacles; the organizer and the promoter; the scientific investigator, who follows material lines. As Jupiter, well aspected, denotes the high-minded philosopher, the worthy law-giver, the sincere and ardent priest, in fact, all who have high and lofty aspirations, so Saturn, when evilly aspected, denotes the narrow-minded, creed-bound sectarian, the materialist, the anarchist, and enemies of society, whether church or state. As Jupiter gives the lofty, expansive and benevolent mind, so Saturn, evilly aspected, gives a sarcastic, concrete and narrow tendency.

DIAGNOSIS OF DISEASE.

Its

Prevention and Cure

As the Rosicrucian Fellowship is not concerned with fortune telling, we pass indications of success in business, courtship, etc., and devote the remaining space to diagnosis of disease, its prevention and cure. Parents have an exceptional opportunity and may lay up much treasure in heaven by judicious care of growing children based upon knowledge of the tendencies to disease revealed by the horoscope. The writers rely implicitly upon this horoscopic testimony, and though, in a few cases doubts have been expressed as to the correctness of our diagnosis, because it varied from that of practitioners in personal touch with the patient, subsequent developments have invariably vindicated our judgment and proved the farreaching penetration of Astrology which is as much in advance of the X-Ray as that is superior to a candle, for even though the X-Ray were capable of illuminating the entire body to such an extent that we could see each individual cell in activity, it could only show the conditions of the body at a given moment. But the horoscope shows incipient disease from the cradle to the grave, thus it gives us ample time to apply the ounce of prevention, and maybe escape an illness, or, at least, ameliorate its severity when disease has overtaken us, it indicates to the day when crises are due, thus forwarned we may take extra precautionary measures to tide over the critical point; it indicates when the inimical influences are waning and fortifies us to bear present suffering with strength born of the knowledge that recovery at a specific time is certain. Thus Astrology offers help and hope in a manner attainable by no other method; for its scope is wider than all other systems, and it penetrates to the very soul of Being.

An Important Warning

If letters of fire that would burn themselves into the consciousness of the reader were obtainable, we would spare no effort to procure them for the purpose of warning students on one particular point in connection with the practice of medical Astrology; it is this:

Never tell a patient a discouraging fact.

Never tell them when impending crises are due.

Never predict sickness at a certain time.

Never, never predict death.

It is a grave mistake, almost a crime, to tell sick persons anything discouraging, for it robs them of strength that should be husbanded with the utmost care to facilitate recovery, it is also very wrong to suggest sickness to a well person, for it focuses the mind on a specific disease at a certain time, and such a suggestion is liable to cause sickness. It is a wellknown fact that many students in medical colleges feel the symptoms of every disease they study, and suffer greatly, in consequence of autosuggestion, but the idea of impending disease implanted by one in whom the victim has faith is much more dangerous; therefore it behooves the medical Astrologer to be very cautious. If you cannot say anything encouraging, be silent.

This warning applies with particular force when treating patients having Taurus or Virgo rising or the Sun or Moon in those signs. These configurations predispose the mind to center on disease, often in a most unwarranted manner, the Taurus fears sickness to an almost insane degree, and prediction of disease is fatal to this nature. The Virgo courts disease, in order to gain sympathy, and though professing to long for recovery, they actually delight in nursing disease, they beg to know their symptoms, the crises and delight in probing the matter to the depths, they will plead ability to stand full knowledge and profess that it will help them; but if the practitioner allows himself to be enticed by their protestations, and does tell them, they wilt like a flower. They are the most difficult people to help in any case, and extra care should be taken not to aggravate their chances by admissions of the nature indicated.

Besides, though the writers have practiced medical Astrology for many years and with astonishing success, and though Astrology, as a science, is absolutely exact and infallible, there remains nevertheless the chance of mistaken judgment on the part of the practitioner and the chance that the person whose horoscope he is judging may assert his will to such an extent that it overrules the indication in the horoscope. He may change his mode of life without knowing what would have happened if he had gone on as before, and thus he may be in no danger at the time when the tendency to sickness shown by the horoscope arrives, it is cruel to unsettle his mind in any case. Naturally, the young student would be most liable to make a mistake in judgment, but no one is immune, we remember a case that came to our notice last year; one of the most prominent European Astrologers predicted for a client in South Africa that on a certain date he would have a severe hemorrhage of the lungs. The poor man wrote to us for help, but though liability to colds in the lungs was shown, we saw no serious trouble at the time predicted, nor has hemorrhage been experienced in the year elapsed between that time and the present writing.

Some students have a morbid desire to know the time of their own death, and probe into this matter in a most unwarranted manner, for no matter how they may seek to deceive themselves, there are very few who have the mental and moral stamina to live life in the same manner, if they knew with absolute certainty that on a certain date their earthly existence would be terminated. That is one of the points most wisely hidden until we are able to see on both sides of the veil, and we do wrong, no matter what our ground, to seek to wrest that knowledge from the horoscope.

Moreover, it has been well said that "the doctor who prescribes for himself, has a fool for a patient," and this applies to diagnosis of one's own horoscope with tenfold force, for there we are all biassed, either we make too light of conditions, or we take them too seriously, particularly if we investigate the time and mode of death. We remember a case where an intellectual woman, principal of a private school in New York, wrote asking for admission to our correspondence class, "if we thought it worth while, as she was going to die the first week in March." She gave us all the aspects upon which she based her judgment, and as one of the writers had just emerged hale and hearty from similar configurations, she gave the lady in question a good talking to that straightened her out; she told the lady she, (the writer), expected to live to a ripe age. Now that lady is thinking of a useful life, she has learned to forget death. Astrology is too sacred to be thus missused; **let the student forget about his own horoscope and devote his knowledge to help others,** then it will aid in accumulating treasure in heaven as no other line of spiritual endeavor.

When a chain is subjected to strain, imperfections in any of its links become manifest, and the weakest link will break first. Similarly, in the case of the body, there are certain inherent weak points and these are indicated in the horoscope. From the moment of birth we subject the body to a constant strain, and in time the weakness of the various points become manifest as disease. The movement of the planets after birth measures the time when any particular link is liable to break. This motion of the planets in the horoscope is called "Progression." Study and practice of medical Astrology requires knowledge of how to progress the planets in the horoscope, and we shall therefore take up that subject in connection with the message of the stars relative to disease.

Progression of the Horoscope

When the Sun rises in the East the day is young and the labors allotted to each are still before us. Gradually the Sun progresses across the arched vault of the Heavens, and marks the time set for performance of our various duties, for keeping our appointments, for taking nourishment, rest and recreation; and when it has ran its course through the day and has ceased to illuminate our sphere of action, its absence invites sleep until the dawn of a new day shall present opportunities for continuation of the activities left in abeyance from the previous day. If the sun remained stationary in any certain point of the sky it would not serve as a time marker but as it is, all events of our lives are fixed by its progression.

The horoscope is a chart of the heavens for the time when the mystic Sun and Life rises and awakes us from the long sleep between two lives, and we are born in the physical world, to continue the labors of a previous life, to keep the appointments there made with friend or foe; to reap the joy or bear the sorrow which is the fruitage of our former existence on earth, and as progression of the Sun marks the changing time of day and year, as it ushers in season after season in orderly sequence and changes the appearance of the Great World, the Macrocosm, so progression of the horoscope, a veritable "Clock of Destiny," registers accurately when the tendencies, shown by the natal horoscope will culminate in events; it measures the periods of prosperity and adversity; it warns of impending temptation and tells from what quarter it will come, thus aiding us to escape if we will but listen to its warning. The natal horosope shows unerringly weak points in our character or constitution, but the progressed horoscope indicates when previous indulgence of harmful habits is scheduled to bring sorrow or sickness; it tells truthfully when crises culminates; thus it warns us to be on the alert at critical moments, and fortifies us in the darkest hour of calamity, with hope of surcease of sorrow and sickness at a definite time, hence the importance of knowing how to progress the horoscope.

But, some may say, if all is thus foreshown, it argues an inexorable destiny decreed by divine caprice, what use is there then of striving, or knowing, let us eat, drink and be merry, for tomorrow we die. If we were born into this life on earth for the first and only time, to live here for a while, and then pass away from this sphere, never to return, fate and favoritism independent of justice would seem to rule. Such cannot be the case, in a world where everything else is governed by law, human existence must also be reducible to system, and we hold that a reasonable solution of the mystery of life is given by the Twin Laws of Being: the Law of Rebirth and the Law of Causation.

That which has a beginning must have an end, and conversely, that which is without ending can never have had a beginning. If the human spirit is immortal and cannot die; neither can it be born, if it will live to all eternity, it must have lived from eternity, there is no escape from this truth; pre-existence must be accepted if immortality is a fact in nature.

In this world, there is no law more plainly observable than the law of alternating cycles, which decrees succession of ebb and flood, day and night, summer and winter, waking and sleep. Under the same law man's life is lived alternately in the physical world where he sows seeds of action and gains experiences according to his horoscope. These, the fruits of existence here, are later assimilated as soul powers in the spiritual world, birth and death are thus nothing more than gateways from one phase of man's life to another, and the life we now live is but one of a series. The differences of character, nobility or brutality, moral strength or weakness, possession of high ideals or low instincts, etc., are certain signatures of soul power or soul poverty. Finer faculties are the glorious garments of gentle souls wrought through many lives in the crucible of concrete existence by trial and temptation. They shine with a luster which illuminates the way and makes it easier for others to follow. Coarseness of caliber proclaims the young in Life's School, but repeated existences here will in due time smoothe the rough corners, mellow and make them soulful also.

The horoscope shows this difference in the texture of the soul and the aspects indicate how the soul is ripened by the kaleidoscopic configurations of planets in progression, which fan the fires in the furnace of affliction to cleanse and purify the soul of blemish, or brighten the crown of virtue when victory is won, but though the planets show the tendencies most accurately there is one indeterminable factor which is not shown, a veritable astrological "x,"—**the willpower of the man,** and upon that rock Astrological predictions are ever liable to founder; that, at times, is the Waterloo of even the most careful and competent astrologer, yet the very failure of wellfounded predictions is the blessed assurance that we are not fated to do thus and so because our horoscope shows that at a certain time the stellar rays impell us in a given direction. In the final analysis we are the arbiters of our destiny, and

it is significant, that while it is possible to predict
for the great majority of mankind with absolute
certainty that the prediction will be vindicated, because they drift along the sea of life directed by the
current of circumstance, predictions for the striving
idealist fail in proportion to his spiritual attainment
to his spiritual attainment of will power which
rouses him to self assertion and resistance of wrong.

> "Yield not to temptation,
> For yielding is sin."

says the hymn, temptation comes from the planetary
ray; but it depends upon us whether we yield and
reap the harvest of sorrow, or earn the joy of "Him
that overcometh." A beautiful little poem by an
author, whose identity we regret to say is unknown
to us, gives the idea in a most pleasing form:

> "One ship sails East and another sails West,
> _With the selfsame winds that blow,
> 'Tis the set of the sail,
> And not the gale,
> Which determines the way they go.

> "Like the winds of the sea are the ways of fate,
> As we voyage along through Life,
> 'Tis the act of the soul
> That determines the goal,
> And not the calm or the strife."

DIFFERENT METHODS OF PROGRESSION
AND THE REASON FOR THEM.

Besides the physical world in which we live,
move and have our being at the present time, where
sunshine and rain, storm and snow, heat and cold
affect our physical being in various ways, a world
of finer substance permeates the denser matter, and

THE MESSAGE OF THE STARS

finer forces indigenous to that realm impinge upon
our souls, as feelings, desires and emotions, because
the soul is clothed in substance from that world.
Mystics therefore call this realm in nature the
Desire World. A still more subtle substance, an
ocean of Thought, pervades both the Desire World
and the Physical World, and as the mind is com-
posed of substance from that region, it senses the
waves of thought generated by other spirits endowed with mind.

Here in the physical world Time and Space are
prime factors of existence, but in the Desire World
distance is practically eliminated because spirits
having dropped the mortal coil travel with the
speed of lightning, and as spiritual sight pierces
the densest substance, light there is never ob-
scured, so there is no night, neither does heat and
cold affect the soul, hence there is no seasonal
division either, to mark time as definitely as in the
physical world. But nevertheless, there is a certain sequence of events, and in soulflights from
place to place on the globe, we sense the nature of
intervening country in spite of speed, but in the
World of Thought, to think of a place, is to be there
instanter, neither is there past nor ftuture, events are
not separated by time, or places by space, but all
is one eternal HERE and NOW.

As the science of Astrology is founded in cosmic
fact, there are also three stages in the progression
from incipient events in the World of Thought, to
accomplished facts in the Physical World, and there
are two methods of horoscopic progressions pertain-
ing to the finer realms besides the actual movement
observable in the Heavens.

Suppose a pole billions of miles long stuck into
the earth at the Equator, and at right angles to
the poles, then, as the earth turns upon its axis, the
end of the pole would describe a circle in the
heavens; this the Astronomers call the "Celestial
Equator," and the position of a heavenly body on

this line is measured in degrees and minutes of "Right Ascension," from the point where the sun crosses the equator at the vernal equinox. This axial rotation of the earth brings a new degree to the zenith, or Meridian about every four minutes, and by the rules of one system of progression we may calculate how many degrees of Right Ascension come to the Meridian position from birth to the formation of a certain aspect. The intervening degrees are then converted to time at the rate of 1 degree = 1 year.

The other system of progression is founded upon the orbital revolution of the earth, but in this system the positions of the planets are expressed in degrees of Longitude, and measured on the ecliptic or Sun's path, from Aries 0 degrees to Pisces 29. The measure of time is the same as in the system first mentioned: 1 degree equals 1 year, but there is this important difference, that while the earth takes only 4 minutes to turn 1 degree upon its axis, it requires 24 hours to move 1 degree in its orbit.

Thus, by one system of progression all the aspects that govern events in a life of 60 years would be formed in 60×4 minutes, which = 4 hours, or ⅙ part of a day.

By the other system, formation of aspects for the same period of life would require 60 days, or 2 months, or ⅙ part of a year.

Thus coming events cast their shadows before, but the shadow varies in length according to the exaltation of the sphere of life whence it is cast.

From the sublime height of the World of Thought, where all things have their inception in the eternal, the progression of events in a life are silhouetted upon the screen of Time while the infant is still upon the threshold of birth, but the shadow is so short: 1-360 part of a day being equivalent to a year, that an error of 4 minutes in the given time of birth would throw predictions out a whole year. Few people know their birth hour to the second, therefore this system of progression is of little use and little used.

Shadows of events projected from the denser Desire World are longer and more definite; it does not require great delicacy or precision to calculate progression at the rate of 1-360 part of a year = 1 year. By this method an error of 2 hours in the given time of birth would only cause an error of 1 month in predictions; this system therefore gives universal satisfaction, and is most commonly used. In the following pages we shall explain a simplified method of this system of prediction, whereby mathematical calculation of events for a whole life may be performed in one minute by any intelligent child that can add and subtract.

The Adjusted Calculation Date

When a child is born at 7 A. M., in New York, and another at 6 A. M., in Chicago, a third at 1 P. M., in Berlin, a fourth at 2 P. M., in St. Petersburg, and a fifth at 12 noon in London, the Observatory clock at Greenwich would point to noon, at the exact moment when all these children were born, hence though the clocks in their several birthplaces pointed to different hours, the Greenwich Mean Time of their births would be identical:—noon. And as the planets' places in the ephemeris are calculated for Greenwich noon, it would be unnecessary to make corrections; we should simply place each planet in the natal horoscopes of these children as tabulated in the ephemeris. This would be most convenient, but the saving of calculation in a natal horoscope where the G. M. T. is noon, fades into insignificance before the facility this gives in progressing the planets for years subsequent to birth, as required to predict events, for in natal horoscopes where the G. M. T. is before or after noon, the places of the planets must be calculated for each year just the same as at birth, but in horoscopes where the G. M. T. is noon, the lucky person may copy the progressed positions of the planets for any year of life directly from the ephemeris for the year of his birth.

Unfortunately, most of us have not been born at the lucky hour and, if we use the antiquated methods of progression, we must spend much valuable time in mathematical work, but there is a method whereby a calculation date may be found which will admit of copying the planets' places into any horoscope in which the adjustment has been made. By much hard study we have made the rule so simple that a child can make the correction, but in order to render the matter thoroughly intelligible we will explain further.

The planets' places in the ephemeris are calculated for NOON at Greenwich.

Theorem I.

If the Greenwich Mean Time of birth was **before** noon, it is evident that the planets' places in the ephemeris are calculated for a **later** time and also that, as they progress at the rate of a day (òf 24 hours) for a year, they will reach the Longitude given in the ephemeris some day within a year after birth.

Theorem II

If the G. M. T. of birth was **after** noon, it is plainly to be seen that the planets' places in the ephemeris for the year of birth are calculated for an **earlier** time than birth, and that the position there given corresponds to a certain day in the twelvemonth **before** birth.

Furthermore, if we can find the date in the twelvemonth before birth, or after as the case may be, when the planets were in the degree and minute of Longitude registered in the ephemeris, we may use that date as a starting point of calculation instead of the birthday, and as aspects formed during the travel of the planets from the position given on any noon to the noon next following, indicate events in the corresponding year, of life, the same starting date may be used for any year. Therefore, once that adjusted calculation date has been found, no further calculation is required to progress the planets in that horoscope; they may be simply copied from the ephemeris. It is only necessary to bear in mind that the horoscope thus erected does **not** apply to the year **from birthday to birthday,** but from the adjusted calculation date of one year to the same date of the next. There are two methods of finding this date; the first is the most difficult and not so accurate, but it shows the philosophy of the correction better than the second method, and we therefore give examples of both.

We will use the figure No. 15 (found in the back of the book), which is the horoscope of a lady who died of hemorrhages April, 1909, to illustrate how the adjusted calculation date is found, but defer description of the case and its crises. The lady was born April 25th, 1872, Lat. 40 N., 80 W. Long. at 1:30 P. M. We first find the G. M. T. by adding to the local time of birth 4 minutes for each degree the birthplace is west of Greenwich.

H M
Local time of birth ....April 25 1:30 P. M.
Correction for 80 degrees West Long. 5:30
                                     _____

Greenwich Mean Time of birth April 25. 6:50 P. M.

In compliance with Theorem II, we subtract from the birthdate April 25, a correction for 6 hours and 50 minutes which the G. M. T. is after noon. The measure of time used in this system is as follows:

24 hours correspond to 12 months
2 hours correspond to 1 month
1 hour corresponds to 15 days
4 minutes correspond to 1 day

According to this scale we subtract
   from ....April 25, 1872
Correction for 6 hours—3 months
Correction for 50 minutes—13 days
                       .   3 months, 13 days

Adjusted Calculation Date ......January 12th, 1872

We may however, find the Adjusted Calculation date much more accurately and with less labor by the following fourfold rule.

Rule

(1)   Find the interval from G. M. T. to the **following** noon.

(2)   To this interval add the Sidereal Time for Greenwich noon on the birthday, as given in the ephemeris.   The sum of these is the Sidereal Time of the Adjusted Calculation Date.

(3)   When the G. M. T. at birth is **A. M. count forwards** in the ephemeris till you find a day having the required S. T. that is the Adjusted Calculation Date.

(4)   When the G. M. T. at birth is **P. M. read backwards** in the ephemeris till you find the day having the required S. T. which designates it as the Adjusted Calculation Date.

We shall use the same example as before to demonstrate this method.
Section 1 directs us to find the interval between G. M. T. and the following noon.   Please observe this, the **"following"** noon, for all depends upon this being accurately understood.

From ....April 26 12:00 noon
Subtract G. M. T.   ....April 25 6:50 P.M.

Interval from G. M. T. to next noon, 17 hrs 10 min.

By Section 2 of rule:

Add S. T. of birthday
    as given   in ephemeris...................2 hrs, 25 min.

S. T. of Adjusted Calculation date 19 hours, 25 min.

By Section 4 of rule:

As G. M. T. is P. M. we read backwards in the column of the ephemeris giving S. T., until we come to January 12th, 1872. On that day the S. T. is 19 hours, 26 minutes, and the Adjusted Calculation Date is therefore January 12th, 1872.

Thus, by both methods we have arrived at identical results, but slight discrepancies may appear in using the proportional method because that makes no allowances for long and short months, hence the method last demonstrated is more accurate as well as easier. If this lady had been born two hours later, the Adjusted Calculation Date would have been December 12, 1871, and where children are born **late** in the year and **early** in the morning, the Adjusted Calculation Date may run into January or February of the New Year. **It is therefore very important to state the Adjusted Calculation Date by year** also, in this case January 12, 1872.

Now, that we have arrived at the point where we are to make use of our A. C. D. to progress the lady's horoscope and show how accurately it marks the crises, the first application of the date to the horoscope is a crucial point, and the student is earnestly warned to overlook no word in our description so that he may acquire understanding of the principle. Once having grasped the point, an immense amount of labor will be saved, so it will pay to follow our instructions to the letter.

Write in the margin of your ephemeris for 1872 opposite the birthday, April 25th, January 12, 1872. Opposite April 26 write January 12, 1873. Oppo-

site April 27, write January 12, 1874, and so on, as
shown below. Every day after birth corresponds
to a certain year of life which starts on the day
written in the margin, and the planets in line with
any A. C. D. indicate the events for twelve months
from that date.

Jan. 12, 1872......April 25	Jan. 12, 1888........May 11
Jan. 12, 1873......April 26	Jan. 12, 1898........May 21
Jan 12, 1874......April 27	Jan. 12, 1908........May 31
Jan. 12, 1877......April 31	Jan. 12, 1909......June 1
Jan 12, 1878........May 1	Jan. 12, 1910........June 2

The motion of the sun and planets from day
to day is slow, and as we count a day for a year,
we may liken their progression to the short hand
on the clock of destiny, they indicate the year when
a certain condition shown in the natal horoscope
has ripened, and is ready to manifest as an event.
The swift moving moon is the long hand; it marks
the months when aspects culminate in events.
Therefore we divide its motion during the year
commencing with any adjusted calculation date,
by 12, but for rough figuring we may consider
the moon's travel in the progressed horoscope one
degree a month.

Planetary aspects alone do not operate however,
an aspect of the progressed Moon or a New Moon
is required to focus the hidden forces. Therefore
crises shown by t he planets are sometimes re-
tarded beyond the time when the aspect culminated
and we may think we have safely escaped, but the
first aspect of the Moon which excites it will prove
that "though the mills of the gods grind slowly,
they grind exceedingly fine." The finer forces lose
none of their intensity by laying latent in natures
lock-box of events. Sometimes it also happens that
an aspect of the progressed Moon or a Lunation,
(New Moon), accelerates an event before it actually
culminates. Such was the case in the crisis we shall
now describe.

Uranus, Saturn and Jupiter were in 21-22 degrees of Declination at birth; but the effect remained latent until the year 1902, when the Sun reached the same degree. (See ephemeris for 1872 May 25th, which corresponds to Jan. 12, 1902.)

The progressed Sun was then in Gemini 4 degrees, 31 min.; 31 min., short of an exact opposition to the Moon's place at birth: Saggitarius 5 degrees 2 min.

But the progressed Moon on the A. C. D. Jan. 12, 1902, was in Capricorn 9 degrees 27 min., (see ephemeris for 1872, May 25), and traveling at the rate of one degree per month it reached the place of Saturn at birth: Capricorn 11 degrees, 15 minutes, in March, 1902. There it excited the parallels of the Sun, Saturn, Uranus and Jupiter, also the opposition of the Sun and Moon, so that the lady was taken seriously ill with the disease which ended her life 7 years later.

We shall next see what brought about the lady's final illness in the latter part of July, 1908, and terminated life in April, 1909. We copy the planets' places from the ephemeris for 1872, June 1st, into the outer ring of the natal horoscope, for the planets on that day correspond to the adjusted calculation date January 12, 1909, but progress the Moon from the adjusted calculation dates January 12, 1908 and January 12, 1909, (represented by May 31 and June 1 in the 1872 ephemeris), to show what critical places she traversed, and the crises thus marked.

If we subtract the Moon's Long. on a given day from its place on the following day, the difference is its motion during the 24 hours intervening, which correspond to a year of life in progression, and division by 12, gives us its rate of monthly travel.

Moon's place on A. C. D. Jan. 12, 1909.
 (June 1 in ephemeris for 1872)............Aries 17.34
Moon's place on A. C. D. Jan. 12, 1908.
 (May 31 in ephemeris for 1872)............Aries 4.23

Moon's travel from Jan, '08 to Jan. '09............13.11

Moon's monthly travel is 1-12th of the above: 1 degree 6 min. This we add to its place for each month as shown in the following table:

	Aries		
1908	D M	Sept. 12	13.11
Jan. 12	4.23	Oct. 12	14.17
Feb. 12	5.29	Nov. 12	15.23
Mch. 12	6.35	Dec. 12	16.29
Apr. 12	7.41	1909	
May 12	8.47	Jan. 12	17.34
June 12	9.53	Feb. 12	18.39
July 12	10.59	Mch. 12	19.44
Aug. 12	12. 5	Apr. 12	20.49

By comparing this table with the horoscope, we note 3 aspects in 1908, and 1 in 1909, all from the House of death.

(1) The Moon in Saggitarius at birth gives the "Wanderlust," but if means are lacking, and health none too good,—the lady also had St. Vitus dance as a child, when the Moon progressed to conjunction of Neptnue and squared Uranus,—and the Moon, at birth, is cooped up in the 4th House: the home, such desires cannot easily be realized. When the Moon progressed into the 8th House,—which brings gifts and legacies also, and cast a trine to its place at birth in February, 1908, it improved the health, brought a gift from a brother, and caused the lady to travel.

(2) In July, 1908, the Moon squared Saturn at birth and excited his natal parallel to Uranus and Jupiter. This brought an illness, as violent as it was sudden, which forced the lady to abandon further travel and return home, had it not been for the sextile of the progressed Sun results must have been fatal. We shall explain the nature of the illness and its astrological indications when we deal with diagnosis, at present we are only concerned to show how time is measured in connection with events.

(3)   In October, 1908, the Moon progressed to
conjunction of Venus in the natal chart. This, for
a time, alleviated suffering to some extent, but you
will note that from the time of the first violent at-
tack in July, 1908, to the end of life, April, '09, the
progressed Moon squared the degrees between Saturn's place at birth and his progressed position for
1909, as shown in the outer ring of the horoscope.
This made the beneficent action of Venus less
potent.

(4)   In April, '09, the progressed Moon squared
the natal positions of Jupiter and Uranus, also the
progressed position of Saturn. This inimical force
from the house of death, the 8th, ended life.

Transits

The progressed positions of planets are the principal significators of events, but their transitory positions in the space at the actual time of events
strengthen or weaken effects of aspects in the progressed horoscope, according to whether they are
akin in nature or not. The New Moons are particularly potent. These so-called "Transits" are seen in
the ephemeris for the actual year of events.

If the student has ephemerides for 1908 and 1909,
he may see that in July, 1908, when the lady was
taken ill Saturn was in Aries 10, within 1 degree
of a conjunction of the progressed Moon and also
within 1 degree of a square to his place at birth in
this chart. Thus he aggravated conditions.

The New Moon, April 1st, 1909, was in 11 degrees of Aries exactly square to Saturn's place at
birth, and Uranus was conjunct the progressed Saturn and square the progressed Moon. Thus all
stellar influences bearing upon this lady united to
terminate life in the body.

HOW TO FIND THE NEW MOON

Among the points in Astrology which bother the new beginner, is how to find the **new Moon,** the **full Moon, Lunations,** when the Moon is **increasing in light** or **decreasing.** Astrological works frequently use these expressions when tabulating the effects of various configurations. But so far as we know, no explanation has been given elsewhere, and we trust the following may make the subject clear to students.

Each Month the Moon comes into conjunction with the Sun, and this conjunction of the luminaries is called a **lunation or new Moon.** After the conjunction or new Moon, she may be seen in the western sky close to the horizon as a tiny crescent, day by day the lighted surface grows larger, at the time of **the opposition to the Sun** she has **increased her light** to the fullest capacity, and at that time we speak of her as a **full Moon**; she then rises in the eastern sky at the same time as the Sun sets in the West. From that time for another fortnight it will be observed that she rises later and later in the night, at the same time the illuminated part of her disc **decreases** until just before the next conjunction or new Moon, early risers may observe her in the eastern sky just before sunrise as a tiny crescent upon the vault of heaven. Thus the Moon is **increasing in light** from the time of its conjunction or new Moon to the opposition, or full Moon, and from the full Moon to the next new Moon it is **decreasing in light.** The time when these periods commence are shown in Raphael's Ephemeris for each year and each month. The student will notice in the lower section of the right hand pages in Raphael's Ephemeris a column entitled Lunar Aspects. At the head of that column are the symbols of the various planets, and below each the aspects which the Moon makes to that planet are tabulated. For illustration we refer the student to the page for August, 1909, given in Simplified Scientific Astrology. Directly below the symbol of the Sun, and in line with the Planets places for the first of August; we note the sign of opposition. Thus we see that on the first of August, 1909, it was full Moon. The Moon then commenced to **decrease in light** until the 15th of August, on that day the conjunction sign under the Sun shows the lunar aspect which we know as a new Moon; from the 15th of August, until the 31st, the Moon was again **increasing in light,** for the opposition sign in the Sun's column of lunar aspects shows that there was full Moon also on the 31st of August, 1909; thus there were two full Moons and one new Moon in that Month, which is a somewhat rare phenomenon.

If the student wishes to know where a new Moon or full Moon falls in the Zodiac, he may obtain the degree by looking in the column of the Sun's Longitude tabulated on the left hand page of the Ephemeris, next to the Sidereal Time of each day. In the illustrations we have just used, we see that on the first of August, 1909, the longitude of the Sun was 8 degrees and 33 minutes of Leo; as the full Moon which occurred upon that day is in **opposition** to the Sun, it is evident that the full Moon was in 8 degrees and 33 minutes of Aquarius. On the 31st of August the Sun's longitude was 7.24 of Virgo, the full Moon on that day was, therefore, 7.24 of Pisces. On the 15th of August, 1909, the Sun was in 21.59 of Leo, and as **a lunation is a conjunction of the Sun and Moon,** naturally the new Moon was in 21.59 of Leo. Thus by looking at the column of the Sun's longitude on the left hand page of the Ephemeris and the Lunar Aspects on the right hand page, the student may determine accurately the points of conjunction or opposition called new and full Moons.

Progression of the Angles

Besides the progression of planets which we trust has been satisfactorily elucidated, we must also note a similar forward movement of the houses, but these must be calculated by the same method

as when casting a natal figure, save that we use the
Sidereal time for the day which corresponds to the
year for which we wish to progress the horoscope.
In relation to the lady's horoscope we have studied,
the critical year is 1909, and June 1 in the ephemeris
for 1872 corresponds. We bear in mind that birth
occurred at 1:30 P. M., in Lat. 40 N. Long. 80 W.,
for these factors are used in placing the degrees on
the houses just as in the natal chart, the only change
is using the S. T. of the progressed birthday.

	H	M	S
S. T. at noon previous to progressed birth-day, 1909, (see phemeris for 1872 June 1.	4	41	6
Corr of 10 sec. for each 15 degrees birthplace place is West of Greenwich	0	0	55
Interval from previous noon to birth	1	30	0
Corr of 10 sec. per hour of interval	0	0	15
Sidereal Time of progressed birth	6	12	16

With this S. T. we turn to the Tables of Houses
for the Latitude of birth, and may erect a horoscope
with 12 Houses in the usual manner, we may further insert the planets' places on the A. C. D. for
1909, then we shall have a complete separate horoscope for the year, which we may compare with
the natal chart. Some Astrologers use that method,
but we advise another, which we think facilitates
comparison and judgment of aspects between the
natal and progressed position of the planets in a
degree unattainable by any other system; it is illustrated in the various figures used in this book.

We write the natal chart in ink, as that is unchanged during life, we also draw a large circle
outside it, to contain the progressed position of the
planets. These, and the houses we write in their
proper places, but lightly, and with pencil, so that
they may be easily erased and the horoscope erected
for another year without necessity of rewriting the
natal chart.

But no matter how placed, two full horoscopes with 24 houses, 18 planets, a couple of dragons heads, each with its respective "tail," and two parts of fortunes, makes quite a "maze," and if the full galaxy of aspects: including biquintiles, sesquiquadrates and other highsounding nonsensicals are to be figured out the astrologer will surely so lose himself in the mathematical labyrinth that he will be unable to read a syllable of the message of the stars. During the first year of his astrological study, one of the writers being originally of a mathematical turn, had the habit of constructing figures, and tables of aspects, so fearfully and wonderfully made that they beat the proverbial "Chinese puzzle," they were veritable "Gordian Knots," and the destiny of a human being was so tangled in each, that neither the writer who had concocted the abomination, nor anyone else could ever hope to disentangle the poor soul involved. May he be forgiven, he has mended his ways, and is now just as zealous to eliminate all nonessentials from the horoscope, but having been enmeshed in the maze of mathematics, his experience should serve as a warning. Our minds, at best, are but feeble instruments to fathom fate and surely we shall have the greatest chance of success by applying our science to the most important factors, and these are usually the simplest.

If this be granted, the question presents itself: What are the essentials and what may be eliminated with advantage to clear the progressed horoscope of useless, befogging elements?

First, with regard to the progressed houses, only two vital points produce results when aspected: the Midheaven, which is spiritual in nature, and the Ascendant, which is a significator in material matters. We shall treat that subject later, for the present we confine ourselves to the argument that it will facilitate judgment of the progressed horoscope if we leave the ten unessential cusps out, and draw two dotted lines with pencil to mark the progressed Midheaven and Ascendant.

In the second place, the student may readily convince himself by looking through the columns of any ephemeris, that the motion of Neptnue, Uranus, Saturn and Jupiter, during the two months which represent progression for a life of 60 years, is so slow, that they seldom form an aspect not registered in the natal chart. In rare cases where an important aspect is formed, the fact is easily seen, and the planet should then be entered in the outer ring of the progressed horoscope, but in the great majority of cases it is better to leave these planets out, and enter only the progressed positions of the Sun, Moon, Mars, Venus and Mercury.

Transits of Neptnue, Uranus, Saturn and Jupiter are important, and when the student has become familiar with the mysteries of the progressed horoscope, **but not before,** he may profitably write the ephemeral position of these planets outside the progressed horoscope and watch their effect, also the aspects of the New Moons. But be sure, at first, to keep the progressed horoscope down to first principles, for fancy aspects are "the stuff dreams are made of," the warp and woof of astrological romances which fade away into moonshine and leave the Astrologer discomfited. It is comparatively easy to wield the shuttle of imagination with natal, progressed and transiting planets, each set with its corresponding houses, and a multitude of aspects to chose from, but simple judgment based upon the prime essentials of a horoscope is almost invariably justified by events.

In conclusion of our treatment of the method of Progression, two important points must be mentioned: The Midheaven at a given Sidereal Time is the same for all Latitudes, so that two children born at the same S. T. would have the same sign and degree on the M. C., but if one were born in Alaska, and the other in Mexico, the Asc would vary much and change the grouping of planets in the houses very considerably, with the further result that planets which influence the first house affairs in one horoscope affect 12th House matters in the other, etc. Thus the lives of these people would be very different.

The same argument applies to the progressed horoscope of a person traveling North or South from his birthplace. His progressed M. C. remains unchanged, but he receives the forces from a different ascending degree, according to the Latitude where he resides, and the grouping of planets relative to the progressed Ascendant varies accordingly. As examples we may state that both writers have left their birthplace, one traveled 2000 miles West, but is close to the same Latitude as her birthplace, hence both her M. C. and Asc are the same as if she had remained in her native city.

The other writer was born in Lat. 56 N., and now lives in Lat. 32; had he remained in the far North, his progressed Asc., would now be Virgo 6, exactly conjunct to Mars' place at birth, but the Asc of his new home is Virgo 0 degrees, and in this Lat. he will not feel the effect of the Mars ray for a number of years.

The other important point we had in mind is the necessity of being definite in regard to the year for which we progress; perhaps a client tells us that a certain event occurred when he was 26, and another in his 50th year. Such statements are ambiguous, and give no safe working basis. The Astrologer may go home, do an immense amount of work to no use, because he thought the client meant that one event occurred when he, the client, was between 26 and 27 years of age, and a later consultation reveals that he meant the year between his 25th and 26th birthdays. Pin them down to the year, 1850, 1900, or whatever it may be, but never accept a persons age as a starting point.

On the same principle, never predict that an event will happen when a person is so and so old, that also is ambiguous and gives them no satisfaction; give the year and month; never hedge; never predict anything of which you are in doubt, when you are satisfied a prediction is justified, speak fearlessly, **but tactfully;** believe in the stars, and the stars will fully justify your faith.

THE ORIGIN OF DISEASE

It is our earnest conviction, that the less we dwell upon sex, the less we read about it and think about it, the purer we shall be mentally, and also less liable to danger of morbid habits, for these are often formed by overstudy of the sex question, and persons having a tendency in that direction should be discouraged in attempts to discuss the matter at all. In planning this chapter we had at one time thought it possible to escape mention of the subject, but more mature thought based upon much study of health and disease from the mystical standpoint has convinced us that we must go back to the allegorical Garden of Eden for the starting-point of pain and sorrow, as fully explained in our literature. The effects of continued transgression are with us today as a matter of actual fact, abuse of sex is in the most literal sense the primal source of sorrow, disease and degeneracy under which the world is groaning, and in a work of this nature it is obligatory to show the causes so that the remedy may be found and applied. Therefore we shall attempt to show first the prenatal influences revealed by the horoscope as a warning to parents that marriage is a sacrament, and not a license to sex abuse, and that "the sins of the fathers are indeed visited upon the children." At the same time, of course, an innocent child is not born with the tendency to a certain disease, its former living has made it liable to a specific weakness, and for that reason it is drawn by the Law of Association to parents from whom it may obtain a body subject to that particular ailment. Thus parents are only instruments in fulfilling the selfmade destiny of the child. If we thoroughly realize that fact, and can be persuaded to live pure and wholesome lives, so that we may draw to ourselves souls of a kindred virtuous nature, how much better for all the world. To drive this point home, the writers undertake to paint the loathsome picture of degeneracy, that the picture of purity may be the more attractive by contrast.

In this connection we present first figure No. 1, which is that of a boy, now in 1912 about 16 years of age. The 4th and 10th houses, the planets in them and their rulers show the parents. The parent who most influences the life is shown by the 10th house configurations, and the 4th house indicates the one least concerned in the child's destiny.

In this figure Gemini is on the Midheaven, and Mercury, its ruler, is square the Moon from cardinal signs. Neptune is conjunction Mars in the 10th House and square the Sun in the Mecurial sign: Virgo. This establishes well the morbid, neurotic nature of the father, his instrumentality in depriving the boy of the faculty of speech and of coordination of muscular movements; the boy cannot walk, but staggers.

The mother's part is described by Sagittarius on the 4th House. Jupiter, the ruler, is in Leo in conjunction with the Dragons Tail, (the Moon's Western Node), which has an influence similar to Saturn. It is also square to Saturn and Uranus; the latter being in conjunction in Scorpio. This describes her as a lewd woman; degenerate, committed to the dreadful theory of soulmates, affinities; free love and all kindred abuses. These lewd tendencies she imparted to the boy. The affliction to Leo affects the heart, and as Saturn is the embodiment of obstruction, restraint and suppression, we may know

that the heart action is very weak, (had the affliction come from Mars, his dynamic energy would
have caused palpitation). Scorpio has rule over
the sex organ, Uranus and Saturn there gives tendency to self abuse, and on the well known principle that mutilation of that organ affects the voice,
we have in this configuration an added reason of the
poor boy's inability to speak. The affliction coming
from fixed signs shows the deep rooted constitu-
tional nature of the evil, and what may come of
conception during a drunken debauch.

THE GUARDIAN OF THE THRESHOLD

Horoscope No. 2 shows one of the most remarkable psychic conditions we have ever come
across. Its portent in some respects are plain to
any astrologer, but investigation by one of the
writers into this person's past life adds sidelights
and gives depth to the meaning of configurations
not otherwise obtainable, also to the writer, who
made the spiritual investigation two years before
the horoscope was cast, it was a revelation to note
how the mystic facts he remembered so well, were
inscribed in this little wheel of life. To enable the
student to properly appreciate the remarkable case
we relate the story of how we came into connection
with the person, what we attempted to do, and what
actually happened.

In the fall of 1910, a friend told us the sad case
of a young boy confined to his bed, lying upon his
stomach and elbows, persistently gazing at a certain spot in a corner of the room, as if fascinated,
his whole frame continually shaking with sobs and
moans. At request of the friend we visited the
unfortunate boy, and found that the object which
drew his gaze, with a power similar to that whereby
the snake charms a bird into its fangs, was an
elemental of the most horrible type we have ever
seen. Standing by the bedside we directed a stream
of force towards the base of the poor victim's
brain, and thus drew him towards us in an endeavor

to break the spell, but the fiend held the consciousness charmed to such a degree that there was evident danger of rupture of body and soul. We therefore desisted, and, with the fearlessness born of inexperience, decided to fight the elemental upon his own plane of being. But the Elder Brother who is our Teacher sought us that evening, he advised caution, and investigation of the genesis of the monster before we took action.

Research of the memory of nature developed the fact that in its last life the spirit embodied in the youth had been an initiate of the Order of Jesus, a Jesuit, and a zealot of the most ardent type, cruel and unfeeling in the highest degree, yet perfectly impersonal, with no other aim in life save to further the interests of his Holy Order. The health, wealth, reputation or life of others he sacrificed without qualm of conscience, so that the Order was benefitted; he would have offered himself up as freely, for he was sincere to the core. Love was as foreign to his nature as hate, but sex was rampant, it tore his strong soul to shreds; yet it never mastered him, he was too proud to show his passion even to one who could have gratified it, and so he developed the secret habit. It must not be supposed that he became an abject slave in that respect; he, the immortal spirit, fought his lower nature by prayer, castigation, fastings and every other conceivable means, sometimes he thought he had conquered, but when he least expected it the beast in him rallied, and the war raged as fiercely as ever. Many times he was tempted to mutilate himself, but he scorned such a course as unworthy a man, specially when that man had taken the vows of priesthood. At last he succumbed to the strain; vigorous manhood was succeeded by a middle age of delicate health, constant pain increased his mental anguish and sympathy was born of suffering, he was no longer indifferent to the tortures of victims of the Holy Office. Being by nature a zealot and enthusiast in whatever direction his energies were exerted, the pendulum soon swung to the other extreme, Paul-like, he fought to protect whom he had previously persecuted, he incurred the enmity of the Holy Office, and finally, broken in body, but dauntless of spirit he fell a victim to the torture to which he had subjected so many.

By the sincerity of his nature, and his later life, he earned the right of admission to a Mystery School and prepared for the privilege of working as an Invisible Helper in future lives. The Law of Association drew him to birth in an American family who were former friends; and from them he received a nervous organization tuned to the high pitch required for his experience.

Saturn opposes the lifegiving Sun, suppresses the nervous energy of Mercury, and obstructs the Venus, (venous), circulation, by hindering secretion of urine and elimination of poisonous matter through the kidneys which are ruled by Libra, the sign of Saturns exaltation where he is placed in this natal figure. As the planets which he opposes are placed in Aries, ruler of the head, his disordering influence manifests through the brain and mind, as well as the genito-urinary system. The morbid condition of these parts caused by Saturns repressive influence on the kidneys is further accentuated by Uranus conjunction the Moon in the 6th House which indicates the health, under the sign ruling the generative organ: Scorpio. As the horoscope shows tendencies resulting from our actions in past lives, it is evident that the self abuse of this person must bring him to birth under a stellar ray affecting the health in that particular manner, for when the soul has been overcome by any particular besetting sin in any life, death does not pay all any more than removal to another city pays our debts in our present abode. When we return, temptation will again confront us until we conquer our weakness. It is the task of this poor soul to extract the phoenix of virtue and chastity from the burning embers of passion and secret vice. May God help

him and strengthen his arm in the terrible com-
bat. Only Astrology, the Master key of Compassion, can adequately reveal to us the struggle and
anguish of the soul, and save us from the crime of
despising one in conditions of depravity.

The beforementioned aspects were from Cardinal Signs, and Fixed Signs, which indicate that
which is almost unalterable destiny. But Neptune on
the Asc; in a Common sign, Gemini, points to a
condition in the making. He is trine to Saturn,
the afflictor of the mind, and supported by the
dynamic energy of Mars.

Neptune indicates the invisible spiritual hierarchies which work with and upon us, and when
placed in the 12th House it is evident that sorrow
and distress may be expected from them. This
position renders the person liable to be preyed upon
by Spirit Controls, but the trine to Saturn and the
sextile to the Sun, Venus and Mercury, protect
him against influence from outside sources. Thus
he became a prey to the demoniac embodiment of
his former actions; the terrible creature known to
Mystics as "Guardian of the Threshold," which
the neophyte must pass ere he can enter consciously
into the invisible World. This dreadful shape had
drawn its being from acts of cruelty committed by
the man in his bygone life; it had fed upon the
curses of his tortured victims, and gorged itself
upon the odor of their blood and perspiration, as is
the wont of elementals; it was a monster in every
sense of the word. Death of its progenitor rendered
it latent, but in the new birth figure time was
marked for retribution upon the clock of destiny.
When the Moon by progression reached Mars' natal
place in the 12th House, his dynamic energy gal-
vanized the monster into new life, and the troubles
of the poor lad commenced. The hate, anger and
malice stored in the monster radiated back upon
him pang for pang and his negative Gemini nature
crumpled under the onslaughts of the demon. When
we saw the thing it appeared as a shapeless jelly-

like mass with many large greenish eyes imbedded at different parts of its body. Every few seconds a sharp pointed, swordlike projection shot out from the most unexpected places in its body and pierced the poor lad who lay cringing upon his bed. Then, although the monster had no mouth, wherewith to laugh, it seemed convulsed with fiendish glee at the fear and pain it had given. At other times, one or another of the eyes seemed to dart from the monster, projected upon the end of what resembled an elephant's trunk and it would halt within an inch of the victim's eyes; gazing into them with a compelling power of awesome intensity.

There being so many good aspects to help him, it is not likely that he will succumb, and when the Sun reaches conjunction of Jupiter's place in the natal figure and the Moon has passed the square to the Sun's natal place, a distinct turn for the better may be looked for. In the meanwhile the poor soul must struggle alone with its selfmade demon. Had not the secret habit sapped vitality in the former life, birth under a stronger sign would have given greater power of physical endurance and rendered victory more certain.

DISEASE OF THE EYES

This malady is due to rays from certain nebulous parts of the Zodiac: The Pleiades in Taurus 29; the Ascelli in Leo 6, and Antares in Sagittarius 8. When the Sun or Moon are in orb of one of these places, and afflicted by Saturn, Mars or Uranus, or vice versa, when Saturn, Uranus or Mars are in these nebulous parts afflicting the Sun or Moon, trouble is indicated, but if care is taken in the case of children having this tendency to disease it may be greatly modified or entirely avoided. The light in schoolrooms calls for attention on general principles, but where a child has incipient eye trouble the parent ought to request proper placement of the child in a modified light, reading by lamplight or in the dusk should not be

permitted, and windowshades in the home ought
to be of a soothing color. With civilization and
life in cities the eyes have become habituated to
short focus and cannot quickly adjust themselves
to variation of range as the sailors and plainsmen.
When a child's horoscope indicates tendency to
weak eyes, residence in a rural district, if possible,
may be of immense value in preserving the vision,
for exercise of the eye muscles by frequent adjustment of focus from short to long range and vice
versa, will materially aid to strengthen the eyes.
It is a fact, that much eye strain is due to congestion of the ciliary muscle which adjusts the lens
to range of objects and the sphincter muscle which
contracts the iris. Each time that fails to act quickly
too much light is admitted and the retina is hurt.
Life in the open while the child's muscles are still
limber will do wonders towards correcting such de-
fects, and even grown persons may derive vast
benefit from outdoor life provided the eyes are properly shaded at first. Careful osteopathic treatment
of the eyes also has a most beneficial effect of stimu-
lating circulation and limbering the muscles.

It is a well known scientific fact, that sensation
depends on ability to feel and interpret vibration in
air and ether, according to the sense involved. An-
cient seers devised the Staff of Mercury as a symbol
of its effects, and among other spiritual secrets
embodied in the undulating forms of the twin serpents, is also this, that Mercury is the originator
of all vibratory movement. Therefore it is prime
factor in production of sensation and mental processes arising in the consciousness as a result. An
elevated, well aspected Mercury therefore makes
our senses acute and the mind keen, an afflicted
Mercury either dulls the senses, or makes the person hypersensitive; in either case an abnormal state
of the brain mind is produced which causes suffering
according to house, sign and affliction; even the
good aspects of a socalled evil planet, though it
brings out the virtue of that planet, also carries with

it a touch of the darker side because even the best of us have something in our inner natures which vibrates to that phase of the planets' nature.

But, besides this roundabout way of acquiring knowledge through vibrations in the air and ether inaugurated by Mercury and interpreted by slow processes in the brain mind where spirit and matter meet, **there is a direct path to knowledge** symbolized by the staff around which the serpents twine. This is the ray of Neptune, the octave of Mercury, which puts us in touch with the spiritual worlds. But, observe this, the staff and the serpents are not separate, the staff goes **through** the winding forms of the serpents, and thus we learn that in our present concrete condition spiritual knowledge is dependent on the brain mind for concrete expression through the brain mind and the latter is colored according to the aspects of Neptune.

Experience has proved that the afflicted stellar ray from certain parts of the Zodiac already mentioned, interferes with the etheric vibration sensed by the retina of the eye, and thus impairs the physical sight. If, in the same figure, Neptune is focussed through one of these places, the socalled "yellow spot," which is **blind** because unresponsive to the etheric mercurial vibrations is sensitized by the spiritual ray of Neptune, and thus it may be that a person physically nearsighted, or even blind, may view the spiritual worlds hidden from people whose sight is focused by mercurial vibrations. The aspect of Neptune determines the grade and nature of the spiritual sight evolved, as illustrated in various horoscopes herewith. These were picked to demonstrate other points, but it occurred to us that the phase just mentioned is worthy of notice. It may be well, however, to warn students against absurd conclusions, we have not said that everyone afflicted with eye trouble by Antares, Ascelli or the Pleiades is gifted in return with spiritual sight. The lady in horoscope No. 5 is much afflicted physically, but Neptune is out of orb,

and she derives no vision from his ray. Spiritual
vision may also be undeveloped in many who have
the aspect well defined, but in those cases it is in
process of unfoldment, and will yield **easily** to
proper exercises. Where this aspect is a square or
an opposition it is wise, however, to refrain from
any attempt to seek illumination, for in those aspects lurks great danger from Spirit Controls, Elementals, etc., which is amply illustrated in horoscope No. 2, where the opposition of Neptune to
Antares is responsible for the awful vision of the
Guardian of the Threshold. There the physical
sight is not impaired, but in horoscope No. 3, defect-
ive eyesight is shown by affliction from the Ascelli
and like trouble comes from Antares in No. 4. In
one the trine from Neptune produces voluntary vision, of the superphysical realms, and in the other his
focus is square, hence the spiritual sight obtained is
intermittent and not under control.

We have spoken of Mercury as originator of all
sense vibrations: auditory, olfactory, visual, etc.,
and of Neptune as its octave; to forestall questions
we may say that in the spiritual world separateness
ceases, sensations merge, so that sound and sight,
voice and vision are one. The Neptune ray carries
both, but undeveloped seers suffering from the in-
voluntary faculty, "see" or "hear" as it suits the
entities which obtain admission to them through
the ray of Neptune.

Horoscope No. 3 shows the inimical influence of
the nebulous spot in Leo 6, the Ascelli, on the sight.
This dangerous degree was rising at birth with the
Moon in close conjunction, and the Sun also in
orb. Saturn in 24 degrees of Libra is just within
orb of a square to the Sun in Leo 0 degrees, and
as a result of these various afflictions the person is
compelled to use bifocal glasses. There is a com-
pensating advantage however, Neptune in eleva-
tion and trine to the Ascelli (with Sun, Moon and
Ascendant in orb), has endowed him with spiritual
sight over which he has perfect control, as the

student may readily see by examination of Mercury, the best fortified planet in the horoscope. Saturn, by sextile, from the sign of his exaltation, gives steadiness, persistence and concentration; Jupiter by trine from the house he rules, expands the mind, makes it religiously inclined and benevolent; Venus, by sextile, adds kindliness and love of beauty. Thus it is evident that in this horoscope the relation of Mercury and its octave, Neptune, to physical and spiritual expression of mind, is well illustrated. Neptune is most highly elevated and Mercury is most strongly aspected. Neither is afflicted, therefore he is not liable to hallucinations, but weighs his experiences in the scale of logic. Compare this horoscope with that of the poor young man afflicted by the Guardian of the Threshold (No. 2), where Neptune is in the 12th house in conjunction with Mars, where Mercury is afflicted by the opposition of Saturn, all from Cardinal signs, contrast of the two figures will bring out some fine points.

In horoscope No. 5 we see the Moon in the 6th house, about three degrees from Antares, and Saturn is in the 12th house within four degrees of an opposition to Antares, about 7 degrees from exact opposition to the Moon; thus his natal influence was minimized. Had the opposition been close or exact, blindness from birth would have been inevitable, but fortunately it . was a weak aspect and the vision was not seriously affected until the Sun by progression entered the 12th house, passed the opposition to the Moon; then opposition to Antares and arrived at conjunction with Saturn. These points of contact in the horoscope marked crises in the disease of her eyes. Saturn being the afflictor, and Mercury also squaring the ascendant, the nerves and muscles crystallized until sight of one eye was lost and the other eye is almost blind. In November, 1912, the Moon will have progressed to the square of the Sun's place at birth. That is the final crisis which will vivify the beforementioned aspects. We cannot restore organs which have been removed before we were requested to aid, and are handicapped by being called so late in the day, but we are nevertheless concentrating every effort to bring the poor lady past that aspect; and there is every indication that, with God's help, we may save her from the awful fate of total blindness. Neptune makes no aspect to the points of the Zodiac mentioned, hence the spiritual sight is deeply dormant.

Horoscope No. 4 is the most afflicted of all, the Dragon's Tail, the Sun and Antares are in conjunction. That alone is sufficiently severe; the condition is further aggravated, however, by a close square of Neptune and Mars, and then the measure of affliction to the eyes is helped by a conjunction of Saturn to the Pleiades which occurs in the 12th house. Thus this horoscope shows the person then born to have very weak eyes, and as a matter of fact, she can scarcely read even when holding book or paper a few inches from the eyes and using a magnifying glass; but the square of Neptune to Antares has opened her spiritual senses to a certain extent so that she hears spirit voices and at times has visions. These manifestations, being uncontrolled by her, are very unsatisfactory of course, but prove the effect of Neptune aspecting these points in the Zodiac.

THE DRAGON'S "HEAD" AND "TAIL."

As it has often been a sore puzzle to students what are the Dragon's "Head" and "Tail" (called the Moon's nodes in the ephemeris), and why one is supposed to be good and to further all which comes under its benefic ray, while the other is considered extremely evil, it may be well to show the reasonableness of the philosophy.

First, let us say for the information of students not versed in astronomical terms, that "nodes" are points where a planet, traveling in its orbit, crosses the Sun's path; as for instance the earth does at the equinoxes, and there is a close correspondence between the precession of the equinoxes, which is explained from both the astronomical and the mystic sides in our "Simplified Scientific Astrology," second edition, and the revolution of the Moon's Nodes.

Speaking from the convenient geocentric viewpoint, the Sun crosses its Eastern Node each year at the Vernal equinox, 50 seconds of space in advance of the point where it crossed the previous year; as the Sun travels 15 degrees per hour, 50 seconds of space are traversed in about 3 seconds of time.

The Moon rises about 50 minutes later each night, applying the same measure, 50 minutes of time correspond to about 3 minutes of space, and the Moon's nodes recede just that much every day.

Thus the Sun travels around the circle of the Zodiac in one year, but requires 27 times as many thousands, (27,000 years), to complete the precession of its nodes: the equinoctial points. The swift moving Moon circles the Zodiac in 27 days and its nodes make a full revolution in 1000 weeks or 19 years. (These figures are only approximate).

In the case of the Sun the place where it crosses the earth's equator in the East is always regarded as the first point of Aries, no matter where in the Constellations it falls because of precession. This procedure is perfectly justified because the life giving qualities ascribed to the Sun in Aries are observable as soon as it has crossed the equator; then the seeds sprout; the mating season commences and the whole creation seems stirred by the solar ray to bring forth. Therefore astrologers say the Sun is exalted in Aries, and Aries is understood to be the first 30 degrees from the equinoctial point, the

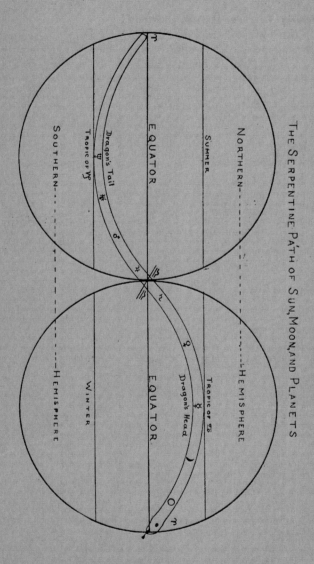

THE SERPENTINE PATH OF SUN, MOON, AND PLANETS

Eastern node of the Sun, where he crosses the equator at the vernal equinox.

On the same principle the Western node of the Sun, the point where he leaves the Northern hemisphere for the Winter months, is called the first point of Libra, and Saturn, the planet of obstruction and suppression is here exalted; he is the reaper with his scythe, he mows down the fruits of the solar ray, he suppresses life and joy, the gladsome voices of our feathered friends are hushed in his presence, and the earth goes down to its wintry grave under his withering influence.

As the Moon gathers and reflects the solar light upon earth, this borrowed light is similar to the direct ray in certain respects, no matter where its Eastern node (called the Dragon's Head), falls in the signs, the effect upon affairs wherewith it is connected, by conjunction is like that of the Sun in Aries, which makes nature sing with joy; it furthers and accelerates personal matters in a most benevolent manner; it so to speak, oils the wheels of life in the particular department where it is conjoined with a planet. On the other hand, the Moon's Western node, (called the Dragons Tail), corresponds to Libra where Saturn is exalted and if in conjunction with a planet it exerts an influence of suppression and obstruction similar in effect to the chill blasts of winter ushered in by the saturnine exaltation.

Horoscope No. 6 shows its part in breaking the femur, (hipbone) of a lady. Its position in the 12th house indicates confinement, the square of the Sun from the Midheaven is a further natal affliction. In December, 1908, the full Moon was in exact conjunction, and Jupiter, ruler of the 6th house (which shows sickness), was in exact square to the Dragons Tail, also in exact opposition to her Sun. Thus indications of trouble were many. Sagittarius, which has dominion over the hips and thighs, occupies the sixth house, so the femur was broken when the lady slipped on an icy pavement just outside

her house.   No. 4 shows the Dragons Tail in conjunction with the Sun near the fixed star Antares
which has an inimical influence on the sight, and
the poor lady who is thus affected is in great danger of blindness.

The Moon's nodes are tabulated in the upper
right hand corners of Raphael's ephemeris; the position being given for every other day; its place at
birth is found by simple proportion, and the diagram
herewith will explain that these points are called
"the Dragon's Head" and "the Dragon's Tail" because the paths of Sun and planets appear serpentine when drawn upon a plane surface.

DISEASE OF THE EARS

The twelfth house indicates the confining influences in life.   Mercury there in conjunction with
the Sun limits the spirit, and deafness hampers its
search after knowledge. The same happens if Saturn,
Mars, Uranus and Neptune afflict, also when the
Mercurial signs, Gemini and Virgo, are on the
twelfth cusp and Mercury is afflicted, (no matter
where in the figure it is placed).   We append horoscopes of people who are suffering from this malady; number 7 is the horoscope of a lady who is
gradually losing her hearing.   Mercury, Venus and
the Sun are in close conjunction in Pisces, the
twelfth sign, which is in the twelfth house.   Blood,
lymph, and the invisible vital fluid, called "nerve
force" by science, are the builders of our bodies;
each planet, except Uranus and Neptune, has dominion over one of their constituent parts.

Mercury rules the nerves, particularly the
cerebro-spinal system, and the invisible rose
colored vital fluid which flows in the visible
nerve sheath.

The Moon also rules the nerves in a general way, but has special dominion over the
nerve sheaths of the body, the sympathetic system, and the lymph.

Jupiter governs   the   arterial   circulation,

Venus rules the venous blood, **Mars** rules the iron in the blood, and the **Sun** rules the oxygen.

Saturn has dominion over the mineral deposits, carried by the blood, which cause the arteries to harden.

When a planet is in very close conjunction to the Sun, three degrees or less, it is said to be **"combust;"** its ray is, so to speak, burned up in the terrific heat of the Sun, and thus the afflicted planet is unable to properly exercise its function in the life of persons born under that configuration. It is also evident that as the weakest link of a chain is the first to give, so the disability would show itself in a part of the body also otherwise afflicted.

Horoscope No. 7 has both Venus and Mercury combust in the twelfth house; we may therefore conclude that there is a lack of nerve force or vital fluid, and that the venous circulation of the ear is obstructed. Thus congestion is inevitable, and the hearing becomes less and less acute. Osteopathy is excellently equipped to deal successfully with a case like this; were the configuration in a fixed sign we might not feel optimistic, but **"Flexibility"** is the salient characteristic of the Common Signs, so we see no reason why with patience and perseverance a cure may not be consummated.

As said, Saturn rules the earthly mineral matter carried by our blood; from this concretions are formed in the softer tissues, also the bony structure. Therefore the skeleton is also under the dominion of Saturn.

In Horoscope No. 8, the auditory disability comes through the fixed signs Leo and Scorpio, this makes it more difficult to remedy, particularly as Saturn is the afflictor and throws his malefic ray upon Mercury from an angle. Science thought at one time that the tympanum was the only, or at least the main, factor in hearing, but realizes now that as much and more, depends upon the timbre of the bony structure. It is the nature of Saturn to obstruct and as Scorpio rules the organs of excretion, we may easily see that this important function is impaired, and that waste products have difficulty in passing kidney and colon. The whole system becomes clogged in consequence, and as Mercury in the twelfth house marks the ears as weak, it is only natural that the auditory nerve becomes clogged and the bony parts of the ear grow denser in the course of time.

Sour milk or buttermilk has a particularly wholesome influence in clearing up a clogged system. Many people rebel against the use of milk in quantity because of an idea that it aggravates constipation; that is true in the beginning, but after a short time the system will accommodate itself to the diet, which will be then found superlatively cleansing, wholesome, and nutritious. Greens and fruits will also aid a person afflicted as horoscope No. 8 to eliminate the waste and effect a cure in time.

DISEASE OF THE VOCAL ORGAN

Among the subjects germane to thorough knowledge of Astrology is the similar effects of intrinsically opposite factors; Saturn is called evil, and Jupiter good, but when Saturn is well fortified in a horoscope it has an exceedingly desirable effect, and an afflicted Jupiter is the very reverse of beneficial. Thus there is a good side to each so-called "evil" planet, and every "good" planet has also an undesirable phase. The signs of the Zodiac are said to rule certain parts of the body, but each sign has also subsidiary dominion over the part ruled by its opposite sign; affliction of Gemini may cause bronchitis, or weaken the arms and shoulders, but Sciatica, a Sagittarius disease, may also result. Taurus rules the throat, it has great sympathy with Scorpio, the sign that rules the generative organ, hence we note the change of voice in boys at the time of puberty; also woman, when she forsakes the path of chastity and lives a life of debauch acquires a coarser voice. Taurus rules the larynx, but Mercury governs the air which stirs the vocal cords to vibration; thus organic affliction is indicated by affliction of Taurus and Scorpio, but functional disability by the position and aspect of Mercury. There is a similar relation between Taurus, (ruling the vocal organs), and Mercury, (ruling the air which passes through the larynx), as between instrument and player. If Taurus (and Scorpio) are unafflicted the vocal organ is in good condition, but an afflicted Mercury may nevertheless cause a functional disorder of the speech. The reverse may also happen, namely, that a well fortified Mercury partially overrides the effect of a Taurus affliction. This is well exemplified in horoscope No. 9; Saturn, Neptune, and the Sun conjoined in Taurus cause a throat affection, but Mercury is in a sign of voice, Gemini, (Libra and Aquarius are the other signs of voice) and in conjunction with Jupiter. The lady suffers constantly from throat trouble, but as a good musician draws melody from a dilapidated instrument, so, by the aid of her well placed Mercury, this lady is enabled to express herself better than many whose vocal organs are sound; in fact, she teaches elocution.

Horoscope No. 3 has a singularly well fortified Mercury, there is no affliction to Taurus or Scorpio, and the gentleman has a powerful voice capable of filling the largest halls without effort, yet not too loud for the smallest, but Mercury in Leo, a beastial sign, and Saturn in Libra, a sign of voice, are obstructive of perfect vocalization, therefore the gentleman has at times a certain halt or hesitancy of speech.

It follows as a matter of course that disabilities of speech are more easily remedied than those that are organic; patience, practice of vocal and breathing exercises such as teachers of voice culture give, (these are entirely different from the dangerous Hindu breathing exercises) are almost sure to restore normal conditions.

Horoscopes Nos. 9, 10 and 11 have Saturn and Neptune conjoined in Taurus; as a consequence all have throat trouble, and also disorder of the genital organs. Nos. 10 and 11 have both undergone operations for removal of certain parts, and Mercury in Scorpio centers the thoughts of No. 10 upon sex, causing intense torture, as is impossible to gratify the craving. Saturn in a fixed sign is certainly a sore afflictor, the reaper of fruits from a past life, and if there is to be any solace it must come through knowledge of the cause, prayer, and the patience engendered thereby.

DISORDERS OF THE MIND

Before closing discussion of maladies peculiar to the head, mention must be made of insanity, though the underlying causes can only be hinted at in a work of this size, but the student is referred to The Rosicrucian Cosmo Conception for a thorough explanation of the cosmic agencies concerned in building the brain, and a key to the astrological correspondences. Here we only give the essential facts.

The brain and larynx were first built by the angelic host from the Moon, (Luna), who used part of the sex force for that purpose, hence the intimate connection between these organs. "Lunacy" is often induced by misuse of the sex force, and "Lunatics" frequently have a flaw in the speech. When boys reach puberty the voice changes, the speech of a fast woman becomes coarse, and degenerate men acquire effeminate voices. In Italy singers anxious to cultivate a high tenor voice have become eunuchs to achieve their purpose.

Into the system thus built by the lunar host under Jehovah, rebel Angels led by Lucifer, the Spirit of Mars, insinuated themselves, they inculcated passion, sex abuse and rebellion against the rulership of the Angels of Jehovah. To offset their influence our Elder Brothers from Mercury were commissioned to foster reason that man may in time learn to guide himself. All the Great Hierarchies work in our bodies constantly, but the three men-

tioned have particular dominion over sex and sense,
each invests one of the three segments of the spinal
cord. The Sublimely Spiritual Hierarchy of Neptune works in the spinal canal and the cerebral ven-
tricles to awaken spiritual senses which, when
evolved, enable the imprisoned spirit to pierce the
veil of flesh and contact superphysical realms. The
Lucifer Spirits dominate the left cerebral hemisphere which now is our principal organ of thought.
The Mercurians have dominion over the right hemisphere, which will come into activity in the future
and elevate mankind to a higher, nobler plane of
life, give us the power over the lower nature and
make us Christlike. The Lunar Angels hold sway
in the cerebellum which is the instrument of coordination. In this veritable "Tree of Knowledge"
the fight is fought between forces which make for
the emancipation of man and agencies which aim to
keep him dependent, as explained in Rosicrucian
Christianity Series. Lecture No. 14: "Lucifer,
Tempter or Benefactor?"

Such are the teachings which explain the deep
reason back of astrological dictums, and any quali-
fied Seer may easily perceive the various agencies
at work in the human body, such are few, however,
and the student of Astrology has reason to thank
God day by day for the blessed science which is of
greater benefit than any measure of spiritual sight.
Though the writers are firm believers in the law of
Compensation which gives to each exactly what he
has earned, neither more or less, they cannot free
themselves from the feeling that their measure of
spiritual faculties have been heaped and shaken
down, they feel very, very grateful for the privilege
and added usefulness in service which this gives
them. Nevertheless, were the alternative placed
before us involving choice between loss of spiritual
faculties and loss of our knowledge of Astrology,
we should not hesitate one moment, but decide at
once in favor of our beloved science, neither ought
this surprise anyone who will give the matter a

moment's thought.   It is true that spiritual sight, even in its rudimentary form enables us to see the condition of the human body to the minutest detail, and thus affords a much easier means of diagnosis than Astrology, but though it penetrates to the innermost core of the bone, mere clairvoyance is superficial compared to Astrology for it shows only present conditions of the body.   To find the causes which led up to that state and judge of future tendencies, it is necessary to consult the memory of nature.   We should have to do that personally, and this time would not permit, as we are handling hundreds of cases, but a simple astrological figure, which we may commission one of our students to cast, reveals as much at a glance.   There are delineated the causes of mental, moral and physical disorders, it shows accurately the stages which have been passed and the crises yet to come.   It also indicates the direction in which a remedy may be looked for and the most favorable time to administer the same.   It helps people Here and Now, and the Astrologer who lives up to his privilege has a mission so high and so holy that the office of Priest, (in the esoteric sense of the term), pales into insignificance. Let the aspirant to this great knowledge remember that he stands upon holier ground than Moses before the burning bush, when he looks at a horoscope. Through that circle-symbol of infinity an immortal soul is laid bare, and woe to him who dares to look with profane eyes, for no matter how that soul may have been smirched in its pilgrimage through matter, it is essentially divine and as dear to the Father, yes, perhaps even more precious, than the righteous who do not need Mercy and Compassion.   This has been somewhat of a digression, but we have no apologies to offer, for we preach Astrology as a Religion and feel the necessity of emphasizing this phase in season and out, if by any means we may inculcate the reverence in others which we ourselves feel for this divine science.

Returning to the astrological consideration of insanity, and in view of what has been said we may note, that the horoscope shows how, in the spinal canal, rays of the various Hierarchies blend, and Astrology tabulates the resultant mental conditions as follow:

People, not congenitally affected, with Cardinal signs rising, particularly if Cardinal or Fixed signs also invest the Midheaven and Nadir, rarely become insane. The active nature forbids morbid tendencies and blues; disappointment is quickly thrown off and hope springs eternal in the cardinal breast urging to renewed struggle with conditions. It is said that the exception proves the rule, and when Capricorn rises the saturnine rulership gives a tendency to melancholy which under certain aggravating circumstances may provoke suicide, particularly when the ruler is cooped up in the 8th house; as we see in horoscope No. 12. Virgo, a Common sign, devoid of stamina, holds the Sun, Saturn, Venus and the Moon in this, the house of death; it robs the person of joy in life and impels him to end it under stress of sorrow. Knowledge, on the part of an astrologer friend has so far forestalled the calamity, and it is hoped, may save the poor man from committing so grave a crime.

When a Fixed sign rises at birth of a normal child, chances of insanity in later life are so exceedingly remote as to be almost negligible. Specially if a Fixed or Cardinal sign is also on the Midheaven. In our extended practice, we know of no exception, the rigid, set and inflexible nature of the Fixed signs seems to protect the mind under all exigencies of stress.

It therefore follows, that the mentally unbalanced come principally from those born with Common signs on the angles. The intrinsic nature of these signs is "Flexibility;" as a reed in the wind they are swayed hither and thither under stress of circumstances, they have no stamina or stability, and take reverses much to heart, while they last.

Sorrow seems to overwhelm them and balance is easily lost.

It is a distinctive feature of the Rosicrucian teachings that pupils in the Western World must be given a reason for every dictum, so as to forestall criticism, as much as possible, for it retards development every time it is indulged. The Rosicrucian teachings therefore aim to forestall questions at every point by giving reasons for each dictum, so that the critical mind may be weaned away from this attitude. We are ardently looking for the day and reign of Christ, The Friend of Man, we do not know when He will come, no man knows, but Paul said, that when He comes, we shall be like Him. Adverse criticism and skepticism were not traits of His character and anything that will aid to eradicate these undesirable characteristics hastens the glad day of **Universal Friendship.**

The reason has been given in Simplified Scientific Astrology, why the Ascendant rules the body as a whole: It is the place occupied by the Moon at Conception. In the Bible Angels are often mentioned as heralds of birth and their lunar home is the focus whence the spirits enter our terrestrial sphere on their return to physical life. They fashion the etheric mould for our present instrument, and direct the growth of the foetus. Therefore, the Ascendant and the Moon show the organic disabilities which lead to mental disorder. The congenital idocy resulting from lack of proper adjustment between the vital body and the physical vehicle has been thoroughly described in the Rosicrucian Cosmo Conception, together with the causes producing the same during pre-natal life. Astrologically this condition is produced by an affliction of the Ascendant, that is to say, the Moon's place at conception; which throws the angle of the Stellar Ray out of parallax to the mother's body, and the physical vehicle is built in such a manner that the head of the vital body is several inches above the skull. Thus the nerve centers are askew, preventing the ego from properly controlling its instrument. This is one of the configurations which produce idiocy and St. Vitus Dance. Uranus and Neptune, are especially concerned in producing this latter phenomenon.

Saturn is the cause of melancholy and depression. Mars and Uranus produce the muscular and violent forms of insanity. Horoscopes 13 and 14 illustrate these peculiarities. No. 13, also shows the connection between puberty and the mental state. Gemini is rising, with Taurus and Mars intercepted in the sixth and twelfth houses, from whence come disease and confinement. The Moon is in Taurus, which rules the larynx, she is in conjunction with Neptune, square to Mercury; and Mars is in Scorpio, which rules the generative organ. There we have at once the tendencies to a disease, which is further accentuated by the fact that Neptune in Taurus squares the Sun in Leo, and Leo has rule over the heart, and is the prime factor in circulation upon which the life of the body depends; thus the threatened illness may be set down to trouble with the blood, produced by a nervous affection. Puberty occurs at the time when the Moon is in the opposite quarter from its place of birth. She entered Scorpio, the opposite of Taurus which held her at birth, at the time when the child was nearly twelve years of age. Up to that time the little girl had been bright, but the conjunction with Mars in Scorpio precipitated the period and robbed the growing child of vitality sorely needed at that time. The initial periods were few, but left her depleted of strength to withstand the square to Mercury and the opposition of the Moon to its radical place. (The radical place of a planet is its position at birth). This affliction of Mercury, the ruler, by the Moon at birth, was thus excited and insanity showed itself in consequence. As the affliction comes from fixed signs, we may judge that it will be impossible to overcome; and the best that can be done for the poor soul is to pray for the day of its release, that it may have a better chance in a future embodiment.

Number 14 is the horoscope of a young man. The common sign, Gemini, is rising. The ruler Mercury is in the 8th house, the house of death; Uranus and the Moon are in opposition. This configuration which is similar to that of horoscope No. 12, has the same significance, it presages suicidal tendencies under nervous strain, and this augur is all the more dangerous as it comes from fixed signs. Mars and Neptune in Taurus gives a desire for drink and the Sun in a watery sign accentuates the tendency. Under such conditions the man has several times tried to end his life in a most extraordinary manner. Jupiter in Sagittarius, square to Saturn in Pisces, increases the looseness of his morals and makes him dishonest. He will forge and steal in order to satisfy his passion and craving for drink, in questionable society. Leo on the second house with Uranus and the Moon in close conjunction, shows that he spends what he gets in dissolute living.

There is one redeeming feature in the horoscope; Venus in the Midheaven sextile to his ruler, and trine to the Moon. He has energy and artistic ability which, it is hoped, may in time rouse the better qualities and make him a man. But again, we reiterate that with the affliction from fixed signs the obstacle is almost insurmountable.

In conclusion the student's attention is directed to the 3rd and 9th houses, which will also have an influence upon the mind. Planets therein act according to the intrinsic nature expressed in the key word of each.

PULMONARY DISEASES

When we studied progression, horoscope No. 15 was used as illustration to show the various crises which eventually led up to the death of the native. But in order to keep the student's mind closely centered upon the mathematical side, we refrained from delineating the nature of the disease which caused her demise, promising to elucidate that point in the proper place.

Virgo is rising and Mercury, the ruler, is trine at birth; but unfortunately he is combust, a term which has been previously explained as meaning that the heat of the Sun burns up the ray of any planet placed too close thereto. The disease was not congenital, however, although the Moon was square to the Ascendant. But Virgo people, we have seen, are extremely fond of being sick. When once they have had a little pain; they magnify and nurse it and are loath to let go. The square of Neptune in Aries to Uranus caused St. Vitus Dance at about the age of five years, when the Moon passed the opposition to Uranus. This was the beginning of her illness. She afterwards regarded herself as an invalid and nursed sickness. At the time of puberty the Moon was in Gemini in opposition to its place at birth. This excited the above mentioned square between the radical Moon and the Ascendant, it also caused the periods to be irregular and troublesome. The blood must have an outlet and the square of Neptune to Jupiter in Cancer, which rules the stomach, caused hemorrhages when the Moon came into conjunction with the Dragon's Tail in Sagittarius (the opposite sign to Gemini), and the radical square of the Ascendant and the Moon were again excited. Then, also the lungs became affected and the crises enumerated in the Chapter on Progression ended the life.

As we feel that this cannot be reiterated too often, we repeat our injunction to students never to let a patient know that there is any danger or that there is a crisis ahead. Particularly, please remember **particularly,** if it is a **Virgo,** for they have no chance at all if they know what is coming.

Horoscope No. 16 shows the natal configuration of an actress. Sagittarius is rising; Jupiter and the Moon are in close conjunction in Gemini, a Mercurial sign, they are supported by a trine of the

Sun; thus she had a most healthy constitution at birth, so far as the lung power is concerned. Mars and Mercury are also in an airy sign, giving energy to respiration and it thus seems as if this person were singularly well fortified against pulmonary trouble. But Saturn, Neptune and the Dragon's Tail in Taurus in the 6th house, gives a tendency to colds and contraction of the throat. Uranus in Virgo produces convulsive movements of the diaphragm and abdominal region; he is square to Saturn in Taurus, and thus we see how graphically the Stellar Script pictures the tendency to convulsive coughing and hemorrhages which nearly brought the young lady to an early grave, when Mars, by progression, came into conjunction with the radical Sun and vivified the square to Saturn. We rejoice to say that the good aspects first mentioned, enabled the young lady to weather the storm; but close attention to diet, regular living, and above all absolute continence are required to regain full physical strength, for there is much evidence to show that license played an important part in reducing the life forces and robbing her of the needed strength at the critical period.

DISEASES OF THE STOMACH

Horoscope No. 17 presents a number of diseases, but all have their root in an insatiable appetite fostered by the fact that the person is a professional chef. Venus in Taurus gives good taste in food, and the sextile to Mercury in Cancer causes the mind to run in the direction of preparations wherewith to tickle the palate. But the Moon being ruler of Cancer, the rising sign, which has dominion over the stomach, shows that this over indulgence of the appetite will result disastrously. The distended stomach presses upon the heart of which the Sun, our life giver, is ruler. This planet is in Gemini— the sign which has dominion over the lungs—and square to Mars in Pisces. Mars rules the iron in the blood and the Sun gives us oxygen; thus this

square shows that the blood will lack in that life
giving element. The conjunction of the Sun with
Uranus in Gemini produces spasmodic motion of
the lungs and labored inspiration to obtain sufficient
Oxygen wherewith to nourish the system; thus we
have the condition called Asthma. Saturn and Jupiter are in Virgo which rules the abdomen, square
to the Sun and Uranus in Gemini, showing lack of
circulation and a tendency to ulcerous growths;
and there is a general lack of nutrition in the whole
system because of the great energy required to eliminate waste from the enormous quantities of food
which this person consumes. Sad to say, however,
persons in that occupation protest that they cannot help tasting, and that in spite of all ills they
must eat to excess. It were wiser, of course, to
seek another profession and train the system to
moderation.

In horoscope No. 18, we have the natal configurations of another chef, they are similar to those delineated in No. 17. Cancer, the sign of the stomach,
is rising, with Mars and the Sun close to the Ascendant; thus the forces of this individual will be directed principally toward the stomach, and the opposition of the Moon shows disastrous results which
eventually resulted from gratifying his ravenous appetite. The Sun is Life and Motion, Mars is dynamic energy, and the excessive activity centered in
the stomach to take care of digestion, causes this
organ to be inflamed. Nature is not a jerry builder,
she builds substantially and well, or our bodies
could never stand the abuse we give them as well
as they do; but even the healthiest organism must
give way in time under such dreadful strain. As
indicated by the Sun and Mars, an ulcer developed
from the heat, it ate through the stomach and re-
lieved the poor soul from its misused body. Neptune in Taurus, the sign of the palate, was of course
also a contributing factor. It is not to be supposed
however, that any one who has Cancer rising or
many planets in Cancer, is necessarily going to die

of the disease to which that name has been given; but it would be the part of wisdom to train children with such afflictions to abstain from over eating, for it is a truism that more people die from over eating than from starvation.

DISEASES OF THE HEART

As the heart is the seat of physical life, its natural ruler is the Sun and the solar sign Leo. But it is a mistake to think that palpitation of the heart is necessarily shown by an affliction to the sign Leo. Indeed, there are many cases where over indulgence of the appetite indicated by the sign Cancer distends the stomach, which presses upon the heart producing what the person then believes to be heart trouble. This was the case in horoscopes No. 17 and 18, both believed their heart trouble to be the primal cause of the illness under which they were suffering; while in reality it was only one of the effects.

But No. 3 shows a case of organic weakness of the heart. The Sun is at home in the fixed sign Leo and receives a square from Saturn the reaper; thus it is evident that the heart was a weak link in the constitution and would cause trouble in time, unless care was taken. Unfortunately, of course, parents knew less of Astrology a generation ago than today, when the science is coming to the fore. The energy, of which this horoscope is full, was allowed to spend itself unrestrained with no thought given to coming disaster.

Venus and Jupiter, the planets ruling the venous and arterial circulation, are in opposition. Venus is in Gemini the sign of the lungs; when the Sun progressed to the square of Venus radical place, and Uranus, transited the sixth house, illness began, breathing became labored as indicated by the square of the life giver to the lungs. Uranus in opposition to his natal place in Cancer, produced the convulsive movement known as a stomach cough, and thus for years this illness robbed the man of vital energy, but these afflictions passed and because of attention to right living the system has been left none the worse for the experience. Moreover, the suffering of the soul has resulted in growth that might not otherwise have obtained.

Horoscope No. 19 shows another case of heart disease. The Sun and Neptune are conjunct in the 8th house, in opposition to Mars. As this conjunction is in the sign Gemini and in the house of death, it is easy to see the portent. The dynamic energy of Mars which tears everything to pieces, accelerates motion, etc., causes palpitation. The Sun and Neptune in Gemini show a likelihood of a hemorrhage of the lungs, resulting from over activity of the vital organ. The Moon and Saturn in Leo show the obstructed passage of the blood, for the keynote of Saturn is obstruction and retardation; thus the valves of the heart become leaky and the backward flow of the blood called regurgitation takes place.

Leo also rules the spinal cord and malefic configurations there may produce hunchbacks and kindred disabilities.

Horoscope No. 20 is the figure of a beautiful boy, well formed and healthy who became afflicted with curvature of the spine. Here we find the Moon in conjunction with the Dragon's Tail in the 12th house, square to Saturn and Uranus in Scorpio. At five and one-half years of age the Moon had progressed to the square of its own place this and the conjunction with Saturn and Uranus in Scorpio, brought on his affliction. After enduring eight years of torture, he died, having been taken from one free dispensary to another and used by the doctors to practice on. Each doctor tried a new cure. He was in plaster casts for years but to no purpose. The mother is represented by Uranus in conjunction with Mars, careless and of dissolute habits; she was glad of the opportunity to place the boy somewhere in order to shirk responsibility of caring for him. The boy died when the Moon had progressed to an opposition of its own place, it was also then in square to Uranus and Saturn.

DISEASES OF THE KIDNEYS

The kidneys are ruled by Libra and Scorpio both. That is to say, the functional activity of secretion of urine comes under Libra; but the parts through which elimination takes place are ruled by Scorpio. Renal stones and gravel would result from an affliction to Scorpio, for they are formed in the peduncle of the kidney. Diseases of the ureters and urethra are under Scorpio.

Horoscopes No. 3 and 21 are examples of how the stars indicate diseases of the kidneys. In both cases Saturn is in an angle and square to the Sun. He is in his sign of exaltation: Libra, which rules the kidneys, is also elevated. This latter point may not be apparent to beginners who look at No. 3 and find Saturn, as they would say, **down** in the fourth house, but the Nadir of the birth place is Midheaven or Zenith of an opposite point on the earth, and planets in either of these points are found to have a greater power.

In the two examples mentioned, Saturn, the planet of obstruction, prevents secretion of urine but does not interfere with elimination of that which has been secreted. But in horoscope No. 8, where he is posited in the sign Scorpio square to Mercury, we have a case where the formation of gravel and renal stones is foreshown by the stars at birth. A person with such a configuration ought to be extremely careful not to drink hard water, for this may cause a painful ailment. Only filtered water should be used for purposes of cooking and drinking. Sour mlik, butter milk and grape juice are great solvents. We may further say that boiling water will not soften it, and the fur which gathers in a tea kettle, where hard water has been boiled, is no evidence to the contrary, for that scaly formation was obtained from the water which evaporated; what remains in the tea kettle for use is as hard as ever.

In horoscope No. 7 we find Saturn in Scorpio square to Mars. Saturn produces the obstruction of the blood known as hemorrhoids, and the dynamic energy of Mars causes rupture of the congested places; thus we have the painful bleeding well known to so many sufferers. As a secondary result constipation adds to the malady, because persons afflicted with the first named disease shrink from the added pain of the stool, and do not respond to nature's call. A prolonged rest seems to be the only physical means which is really effective. Nature, however, will be very much aided by proper osteopathic manipulations, and a diet consisting principally of milk.

HIP DISEASE

Sagittarius rising, or in the 6th or 12th houses, is responsible for broken bones and accidents. Under the chapter on the Dragon's Tail we saw how the person described in horoscope No. 6 fell upon the ice and broke her hip. No. 21 has even stronger indications of accidents and probably the life will end in an untoward manner. Sagittarius is rising. Saturn is exalted in the Midheaven exactly square to the Sun; and Neptune is elevated at the Nadir also squaring the Moon; thus both luminaries are afflicted. As the Sun is lord of the house of death these auguries presage an untimely end. The only hope lies in the sextile of Jupiter to the Sun which gives hair breadth escapes. This gentleman's life has been jeopardized many times in railway wrecks, automobile accidents, etc.; but although he has thus been near the gate of death many times, the benefic ray of Jupiter has so far preserved his life and no bones have yet been broken. The lady described in horoscope No. 22 has not been so fortunate, her arms and limbs have been accidentally broken several times, for Mars and the Moon are in Sagittarius in the 12th house, also in opposition to Jupiter. The Sun and Mercury are in the 8th house in opposition to Neptune and these planets square the first mentioned positions. Saturn, her ruler, is square to Venus so that she attracts accidents and never escapes being hurt.

As we have already spoken of afflictions connected with the generative organ when we considered horoscopes No. 9, 10, 11, 13, we will omit further mention of that subject.

DISEASES OF THE LIMBS

In horoscope No. 7 we find Mars in Aquarius square to Saturn, and from this affliction it is evident that there is an obstruction of the blood in the lower limbs, usually known as varicose veins. Horoscope No. 17 shows Mars in the sign Pisces in opposition to Saturn and Jupiter. It is the nature of Saturn to obstruct, and his conjunction with Jupiter shows that the circulation is poor. Mars in Pisces produces heat, inflammation and swelling of the feet, because of the stagnated blood. We have already seen that the person there described is gluttonously inclined, and therefore, it is no wonder that stagnation of the blood produces such painful afflictions as indicated by these configurations. The remedy, of course, is self evident, it is moderation.

We have now given an exposition of the methods we use in diagnosis of disease. This we trust will enable the student to work out the subject for himself or herself in greater detail. And as he or she uses it unselfishly to aid suffering human beings, the spiritual qualities will be developed in each so that the Message of the Stars revealed in each horoscope will be as an open book. Thus used, this wonderful science will aid him or her to lay up treasures in heaven, as nothing else in the world can do. And we pray God, that this little book may be the means of fostering soul growth in all who aspire to follow the dual commandment of Christ:

"Preach the Gospel and Heal the Sick."

IMPORTANT NOTICE

Despite all we can say, many people write enclosing money for horoscopes, forcing us to spend valuable time writing letters of refusal and giving us the trouble of returning their money. Please do not thus annoy us, it will avail you nothing, we do not advise people in worldly affairs on any consideration.

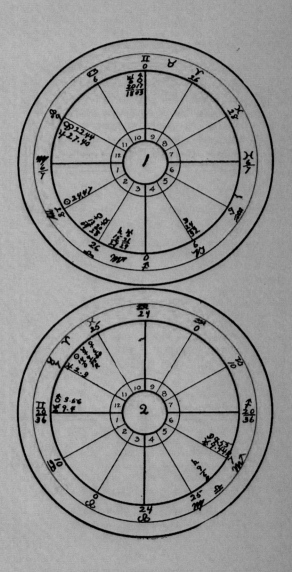

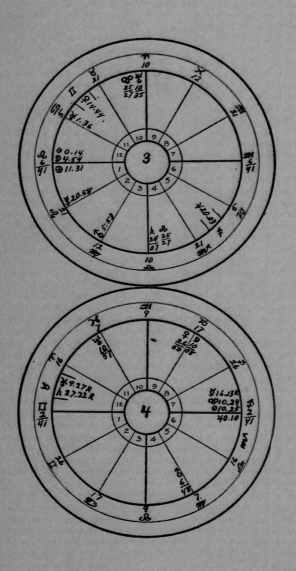

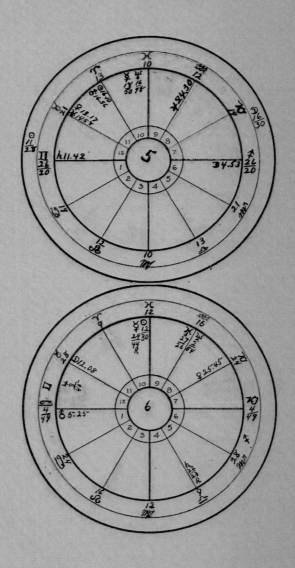

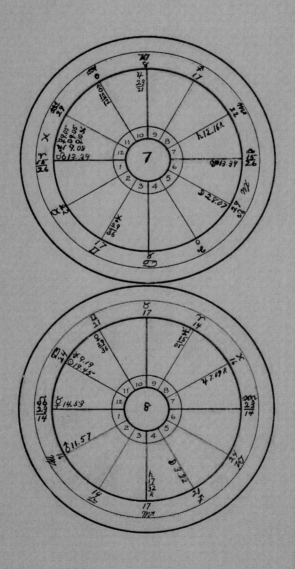

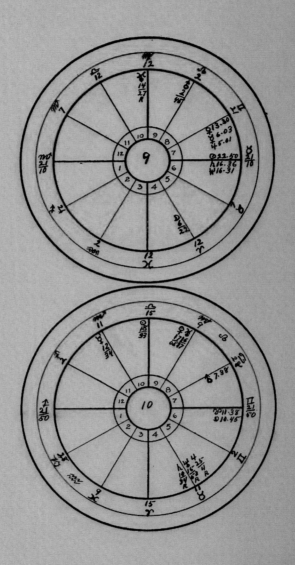

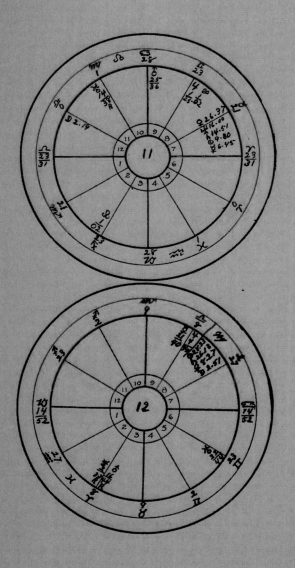

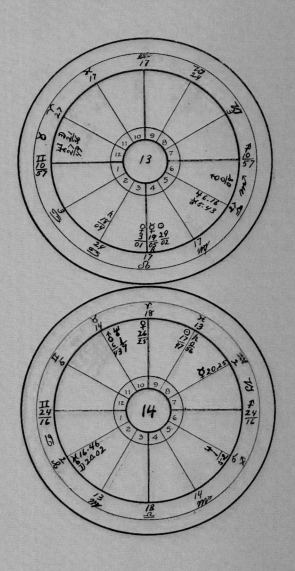

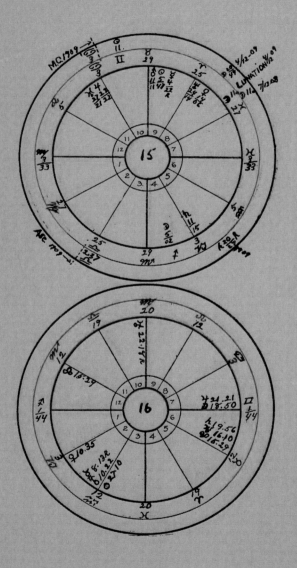

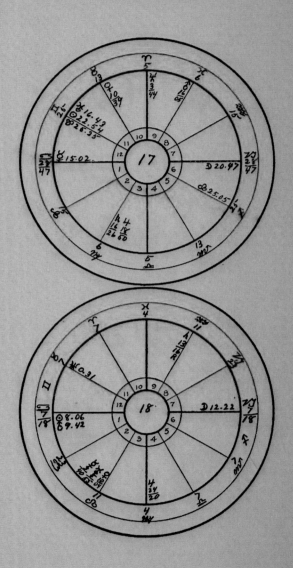

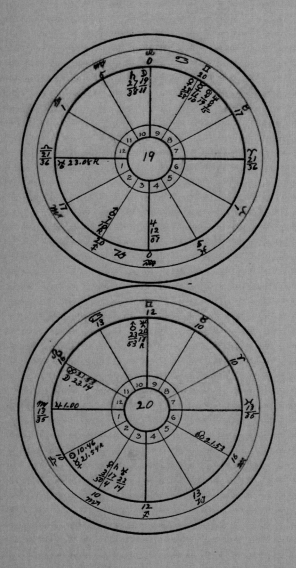

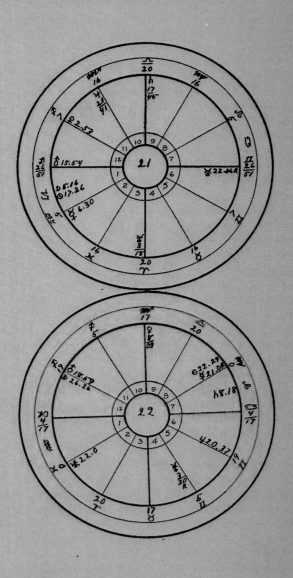

The Rosicrucian Cosmo

Third Edition

602 pp. 12mo. fine clear print, some, durable binding, cloth cov beautiful symbolic design in red, black and gold; edges also gilt. It has 30 tables and diagrams, some printed in colors. Third edition, revised, enlarged and thoroughly indexed for reference, price $1.50 post free.

Three large editions were required to supply the demand for this epoch making book in the first 18 months after publication, and thousands of unsolicited letters attest that students have here found what they have long sought elsewhere in vain.

The Rosicrucian Philosophy.

(In Questions and Answers)

432 pp. 12mo. printed and bound in the same handsome, luxurious style as the above book, price $1.15 post paid.

This is an occult information Bureau; a book of ready reference upon all mystic matters. It ought to be in the library of every student.

The Rosicrucian Mysteries.

200 pp. 12mo. cloth cover stamped in red, black and silver, price 75c post paid.

Specially suited to beginners, but contains much new information about the effect of light and color on the consciousness, and their value in training of children.

Simplified Scientific Astrology.

A complete book of instruction in casting a horoscope, having all necessary tables, replete with diagram, thorough in explanation and full of information not elsewhere obtainable. The second edition has been much enlarged, but the price remains the same as for the first edition, 35c; by mail, 40c.

Simplified Calculation Blanks.

Many good Astrologers are lost to the world because they give up in despair before they have learned to calculate a horoscope, for people gifted with intuition and innate ability to read a horoscope are often poor mathematicians. The Calculation blank does away with all strain incident to calculation; every operation is tabulated on seven typewritten sheets. The student has only to fill in figures in blank spaces provided for that purpose, he cannot possibly err, and before he realizes it, the horoscope is cast. 15c each, 4 for 50c.

Horoscope Blanks 8½x11, with or without index of aspects, as ordered, 10c per doz.

Made in United States
Cleveland, OH
26 December 2024

12618536R10058